LANGUAGE THERAPY

A PROGRAMME TO TEACH ENGLISH

ROBYN E LEWIS and **CLAIRE PENN**

WITWATERSRAND UNIVERSITY PRESS

ISBN 1 86814 087 3

© Robyn E. Lewis and C. Penn 1989

All rights reserved. No part of this publication may be reproduced, stored in a retrieval system, or transmitted in any form or by any means, electronic, mechanical, photocopying, recording, or otherwise, without the prior permission of the copyright owner.

Design and typesetting by Neil Napper & Associates

Illustrations by Brother August

Printed and bound by Interpak Natal, Pietermaritzburg

Acknowledgements

The Witwatersrand University Press would like to thank the copyright holders for permission to include material from the following sources;

D Crystal, P Fletcher and M Garman, *The Grammatical Analysis of Language Disability*. 1st edn 1976, London: Edward Arnold; 2nd edn 1989, London: Cole and Whurr. Laura Lee, *Developmental Sentence Analysis*. Evanston: Northwestern University Press, 1974. R Quirk, S Greenbaum and J Swartvik, *A Grammar of Contemporary English*. (Longman Group UK Ltd 1972). © Quirk *et al.* 1972.

DEDICATION

To Eric, with love and thanks for enduring a diet of speech therapy for breakfast, lunch and supper!
Robyn

To Jonty Levin whose language development inspired the ideas in this book.
Claire

To Gay, Anndrea & Daniel,
With all my love,
Your Ma.

You're all in the book!

CONTENTS

INTRODUCTION 1

BOOK ONE

GUIDELINES FOR ASSESSMENT AND THERAPY 5

1   Assessment – the Baseline of Therapy 7

2   Planning a Session 25
        Play as a medium for learning; controlling
        the interaction; selecting a target; equip-
        ment and design; results and conclusions

3   The Importance of Reception 32
        Parent-child communication as a model;
        levels of linguistic input; colloquial lan-
        guage forms; dialogue

4   Creating Relevance and Context: situational; intentional 35
        linguistic; listener and conversational

5   Motivation 38
        Communication as a motivating force;
        tokens and 'edible' rewards; clarity of
        goals; relevance of the activity and limits

6   Techniques 40
        Expansion; Simple expatiation; Alternative
        model imitation; Pointing out an error;
        Completion replacement; Alternative re-
        placement; Revision; The forced alterna-
        tive; Verbal absurdity; Acting out
        commands; Silence!; The use of one
        modality to cue another; Varying the con-
        text

7 Equipment 48
   Model dolls; Body parts and clothing;
   Model animals; Other props; Mechanical
   toys; Tokens; Miscellaneous containers; A
   floor map; Commercially produced
   programmes; Books and pictures; Illustration of verbs; Story books

8 Home Visiting 55
   Purposes of the home visit: Language en-
   vironment; Family dynamics; Arranging
   for the visit; How to conduct yourself;
   What to look for: the physical setting, the
   neighbourhood, the home, gardens, toys –
   their storage, care and use, pets; Family interaction; Record keeping

9 School Visit 65

   Summary 66

BOOK TWO

LARSP – TECHNIQUES AND SUGGESTIONS FOR EACH STAGE

1 Stage 1: Vocalisation and the First Lexicon 69
   Introduction
   Encouraging vocalisation: engaging in babbling interchange; onomatopoeic words; voice activated toys; use of a mask; use of vocalisation in pragmatic contexts

2 LARSP – Stage I 74
   Minor sentences; Major sentences; The first words

   The Selection of a Lexicon: How to introduce early 75
   lexical items – nouns, verbs, prepositions, adverbs, questions and 'minor' sentences

   Expanding the Lexicon: Classification of 79
   the primary, secondary and tertiary lexicon

   Stories and Books – the increment of the 81
   lexical repertoire; increasing comprehension and the use of grammatical forms; the child's own narration

   Metalinguistics, Reading and Writing 84

3 Stages II-IV – Developing Language Complexity 86
   Some clinical considerations

4 Stage II – Clauses 88
   Activities to teach the listed structures

5 Stage III – Expansions 98
   Activities to teach the listed structures

6 Transition to Stage IV – Expansions 112
   Activities to teach the listed structures

7   Stage IV – Clauses 122
        Activities to teach the listed structures

8   Stage V – Clauses, Phrases, Word 134
        Activities to teach the listed structures

9   Stage VI – (+) New types of construction 140
        (-) Errors made on all previous construc-
        tions

BOOK THREE

THERAPY WITH SPECIAL GRAMMATICAL CATEGORIES: THE PHRASAL COMPONENT

Introduction 146

1   Determiners: The article: the, a(n) 147

2   Pronouns: Definition and description 150
            Indefinite Pronouns: Demonstrative
            Pronouns; Pronouns of number (count)

       Activities for teaching Indefinite Pronouns 151

       Personal Pronouns: personal, reflexive and possessive 160

       Activities for teaching Personal Pronouns 163

       WH-pronouns 171

3   Verbs: Definition and description 178

       Uninflected verbs; Copula is or 's 181

       Auxiliary verbs; form of auxiliary verbs commonly used . . 182
            The auxiliary be; The auxiliary have; The
            modal auxiliaries

       The Passive Voice 187

       Non-finite verb phrases: 188
            Infinitive complement; non-complementary
            infinitives; children's development of the
            infinitive; gerunds and participles

       Children's Verb development: 192
            Irregular past tense verbs used by children

       Activities to teach the Verb 194

       Activities to teach Secondary Verbs 218

4	The Negative: Definition and description	223
	Children's development of negation with verbs; Problems encountered with the negative	
	Activities to teach the negative	224
5	Questions: Definition and description	226
	The interrogative question; The development of the Interrogative Reversal; Teaching yes/no questions;	
	Wh-questions: Definition and description	228
	The development of wh-questions; some relevant aspects of teaching the wh-question	
	Activities to teach wh-questions	231
6	Conjunctions: Definition and description	244
	The development of conjunctions in children; Clinical problems with conjunctions	
	Activities to teach conjunctions	245
7	Adverbs: Definition and description	257
	Activities to teach the adverb as a single word or phrase	258
8	Adjectives: Definition and description	262
	Activities to teach the adjective	264
9	Prepositions: Definition and description	267
	Children's acquisition of prepositions; Prepositional meanings	
	Activities to teach prepositions	273
	Metaphorical use of prepositions	281
	Conclusion	285
	Bibliography	287

INTRODUCTION

The past twenty years have seen the emergence of a vast body of writing in the area of child language development. Within a relatively short period of time workers in the field have been required to make several shifts in framework. Initially this entailed a shift from an approach largely structural in nature, to approaches focusing on semantic theories of language acquisition, and through these to more functional and cognitive viewpoints. Such changes in emphasis have been reflected in the area of child language pathology, where we have observed a shift from the more behaviourally-orientated treatment paradigms towards a greater awareness of the relevance of context.

The effective language clinician should always keep in touch with prevailing linguistic theory, and should be alert and sensitive to winds of change, aware of their implications for the profession. Nevertheless the language clinician should above all be able to assess the merit of these views, and should be able to retain or adapt those approaches which best suit his or her own particular caseload demands despite the whims of the latest journals.

The effective clinician is accountable in many ways. She can, for example, be defined in operational terms as one who achieves rehabilitation in as complete and as natural a way as possible. Primarily the clinician is accountable to the client rather than to a prevailing theory or to textbooks on child language acquisition.

It was from this point of view that the present book emerged. It is written from an eclectic perspective because its focus is therapeutic. It attempts to incorporate the lessons and ideas gleaned from a large body of literature on the topic of child language, selecting those which might be most successful for the practising clinician.

The practitioner dealing with a language-impaired child needs to address three main issues:

      1. What language does the child need to acquire?
      2. When does he do this?
      3. How can he do this?

The final question is the focus of this workbook. We will explore tried-and-tested ways for the development of language in the child with a language delay or deviance. These methods have their bases in two proven assessment and remediation paradigms, but, extending beyond the latter, they also incorporate the knowledge pertaining to social and cognitive domains, which we have gleaned from other diverse sources on child language. This workbook emerged from our perception of a desperate need among the therapists in our community for a structured, effective and flexible framework for language therapy.

The two working models on which our approach is based are the LARSP framework and the Laura Lee framework. These are essentially syntactic models, and we believe that they provide a solid baseline for the remediation of pre-school language disorders. What both of these approaches have in common is that they are syntax-based, stage-based and they focus on the pre-school child. Furthermore their application is variable and flexible, and has been used successfully with many hundreds of children in South Africa over the past decade.

A working knowledge of both the LARSP and Lee techniques is the necessary prerequisite to a sound understanding of this text. It is thus geared primarily to the speech and language therapist who has received a grounding in these methods. However we anticipate that this workbook may well be useful to other professions working with the language of the pre-school child – these include remedial teachers and teachers of the deaf. It may also prove a useful guideline for those teaching English as a second language, particularly in a pre-school setting. Therefore we have made liberal reference in the text to the application of these techniques to populations such as that of the deaf child, stressing that these approaches may be adapted across cultural and linguistic boundaries.

We believe that the suggestions we provide should help the therapist to plan systematic, orderly and effective language therapy. Our methods focus on the areas of syntax, semantics and pragmatics. The latter focus on context is an essential consideration in the emergence, the development and the remediation of language. We believe that the child is a social being whose linguistic skills depend on his cognitive and social milieu. Every language technique which is suggested occurs, as far as possible, in a natural language setting. Such a setting, as De Maio (1983) suggests, incorporates cognitive and social skills too. De Maio's unified model is perhaps the best way to illustrate our conception of this approach.

Our approach to remediation is thus play-based, and highlights in particular the important role of the child's cognitive and social abilities. We do not believe in the recipe-book approach to language therapy. Sadly, this approach appears to be a characteristic of all too many of the currently available, often prohibitively expensive language kits. Nor can we possibly condone the traditional 'Aunt Nelly' approach to therapy so humorously described by Crystal (1976) – that is, therapy based on the successful and charismatic endeavours of an experienced natural therapist. We do however strongly believe in a systematic, orderly, principled and developmental approach to remediation, a controlled system governed continuously by knowledge – a knowledge of where the child is, where he is going, and through which stages he must move to get there.

We do not want this book to join the ranks of many tomes on child language, collecting dust on the therapist's bookshelves. Rather it is our hope that it will collect peanut butter and playdough, two important ingredients of active language therapy! It should be an aid and guideline for the therapist, not a substitute for creative and individualised endeavour.

Note: In this text, the terms 'grammatical structure' and 'syntax' are used interchangeably.
The masculine pronoun 'he' applies to both male or female clients to avoid clumsy repetition of 'he' or 'she', and to avoid confusion, since the therapist, for the purposes of convenience, is denoted by the feminine pronoun.

BOOK ONE

GUIDELINES FOR ASSESSMENT AND THERAPY

1. Assessment – The Baseline of Therapy

Before any language therapy can begin, we need to know the exact level of language development which the child has reached. The assessment or diagnosis of language ability should become a regular and ongoing feature when working with the language-impaired child.

Several alternatives are available to the language clinician who wishes to characterise the language of the child. For example, she can rely on one of the many available standardised tests of language such as the *Peabody Picture Vocabulary Test (Dunn)*, or the *Reynell Developmental Language Scale*. These tests characterise an aspect of language, such as receptive syntax, expressive syntax, or vocabulary. The child's performance on this test is then compared to that of a standardised group. With the exception of the *Test of Oral Language Production* developed by Vorster, there are no tests which have been standardised which are specifically applicable to the South African population. Even Vorster's test has been standardised on 'Whites' only. Hence when we use standard language tests in this country our interpretation is always limited by the fact that we draw on American or English norms.

An alternative way of assessing language – one that has become increasingly popular – is the collection and analysis of a language sample. This involves the recording of samples of the child's spontaneous and interactive language over a period of time, so that one has a corpus of utterances sufficiently large to be representative of the child's language in an everyday situation. Much has been written about the how and why of language sampling, and this will not be repeated here. Interested readers can refer to the following texts which give excellent guidelines on how to collect, elicit and transcribe a language sample:

> J. Miller, *Assessing Language Production In Children*, 1981.
> D. Crystal *et al. The Grammatical Analysis of Language Disability*, 1976.

Our own particular method is that espoused by Crystal and his co-workers: after establishing a rapport with the child in an easy and facilitating environment, approximately twenty minutes of his interactive language is recorded.

During this time the therapist keeps note of contextual aspects, and the sample is transcribed immediately afterwards. The transcription includes all the utterances of the therapist (or teacher, or the person interacting with the child). It is useful to note down intonational aspects as this sometimes helps to disambiguate utterances. The time period of the language sample can be very flexible. Usually twenty minutes with a talkative child will provide a representative language sample. However there are some children who require longer sampling periods. It is also very useful to record the child's language with different communicative partners, and this has implications for our therapy, as we very often notice a difference in the child's language when he talks to different people.

The sample may be recorded in a number of ways. Ideally we should make a video recording since this provides a great deal of extra information about the child's non-verbal communication. Indeed a video recording becomes essential for the sampling of a deaf child's language. The non-verbal communication which a deaf child uses may often substitute for or supplement verbal language, particularly if the child has learned a formal sign language, and if he is interacting with someone who signs. In other cases an audio tape will suffice, but the tester should always ensure that the microphone is of a high quality. The last resort is an on-line transcription, but this is very difficult to accomplish unless one has a child who is essentially non-verbal, or who is at the very first stage of language development.

At this stage it seems appropriate to make special mention of the difficulties encountered in collecting a language sample from a young deaf child who either has very little verbal language, or whose speech is so unintelligible as to make transcription difficult if not impossible. A child with multiple phonological disorders may also fall into this category. In such cases the only way to estimate the language level of the child is to rely on a highly structured framework of elicitation, such as elicited imitation. The GAEL test developed specifically for assessing the language of the deaf child is useful here, although one may devise one's own stimuli to ascertain the language level which the child has attained. Our own paradigm with these children has always been a 'test-teach-test' paradigm. Through some trial therapy we are best able to determine the child's expressive and receptive competence. It should be remembered that there may be a discrepancy between the child's level of understanding of oral language and his level of language production. Similarly in the young deaf child we may find a significant difference between the level of competence at a signing level, and the level of competence at an oral language level.

To return now to the child who does have spontaneous language – many therapists complain that the transcription of a sample is too tedious and time-consuming to warrant the effort. Indeed with a talkative child the transcription may well run into several pages. Certainly this method is more time-consuming than the administration of a standard test, but then in our opinion we are gaining considerably more information about the child, and have a clear baseline from and upon which to plan our therapy – a point which we hope will become apparent later.

After transcription comes the analysis of the language sample. There are many ways to undertake this analysis. In the literature of child language one finds analyses ranging from word counts to calculations of mean sentence length, to considerations of the range of different parts of speech.

The method we will describe here, which is an analysis of the syntax or grammar of the language, is again that described by Crystal. This method of analysis was developed in 1976 and is based on the Quirk *Grammar of Contemporary English* (GCE). Essentially GCE recognises certain discrete levels of description: the sentence; the clause; phrase levels and word levels. Briefly:

> Sentences may be divided into major sentences (having a subject/predicate structure), or minor sentences (without this structure). Major sentences may be simple (in that they contain one clause only), or multiple (with clauses combined either by the process of co-ordination or by means of subordination).
>
> The elements of a clause are subject (S), verb (V), complement (C), object (O) or adverb (A). These elements may be combined in a number of different ways, such that the basic structure may be summarised as follows:
>
> $$SV + \begin{Bmatrix} O \\ C \\ A \end{Bmatrix} + \begin{Bmatrix} O \\ C \\ A \end{Bmatrix} + (A)$$
>
> Each element of the clause structure consists in itself of component parts which are thus known as phrase structure components. For example, the subject or object of a sentence may be a pronoun, a noun phrase, a dependent clause or a prepositional phrase. The complement may be realised on the phrase level as an adjectival construction, the adverbial as a prepositional phrase, and the verbs as a verb phrase consisting of main and auxiliary verbs.

Aspect of the Grammar	Abbreviations	Example
Clause Structure Elements:		
Subject	S	*The boy* ran away.
Verb	V	We *ate* his pudding.
Object	O	John passed *the ball*.
Direct	Od	We gave the girl *an apple*.
Indirect	Oi	She gave *the boy* a pear.
Complement	C	She seems *much happier*.
Adverbial	A	They were *in the kitchen*.
Phrase Structure Elements:		
Noun Phrase	NP	*The girl I saw yesterday* is here.
Determiner noun	DN	The room
Adjective noun	AdjN	Blue box
Initiator	I	*Some of them* are present.
Postmodification:		
Prepositional phrase	PrDN	The man *in the garden*
Dependent phrase		The boys *walking down the road*
Verb Phrase	VP	He *might have to be asked*.
Copula	Cop	He *is* happy.
Auxiliary	Aux	He *is* run*ning*.
Particle	VPart	He *looked over* the room.
Negative	NegV	He *won't come* on Tuesday.
Word Structure:		
Noun Phrase		
Plural	Pl	The dog*s* bark.
Genitive	gen	The dog*'s* bone.
Comparative	er	bigg*er*
Superlative	est	bigg*est*
Verb Phrase		
3rd person singular	3s	He eat*s*.
Present participle	ing	eat*ing*
Past participle	en	have be*en*
Past tense	ed	jump*ed*, ran
Contracted auxiliary	'aux	he*'s* coming
Contracted copula	'cop	he*'s* clever
Contracted negative	n't	ca*n't* walk
Adverbial marker	-ly	beautifu*lly*
Sentence Connectivity		
Co-ordination	SVA c SVA	John came at three *and* we came later.
Subordination	SVA s SVC	Mary ran home *because* she was late.
Sentence Types		
Statement		
Questions		
Yes – No	VS	Can he come?
wh-	QVS	When did he come?
Commands		
Let	Let XY	Let Jane do this.
Do	Do XY	Do come in.
Exclamations		
What		What a lovely day!
How		How tiring it is!

Table 1: Aspects of Quirk's *Grammar of Contemporary English* – the authors' tabulation of the *GCE* structuring of English grammar

Consideration is also given to word structure applicable to the noun phrase (for example plural endings, comparative endings); to the verb phrase (for example tense markers such as -ing, -en and -ed); and to adverbs (marked by -ly). Four major functions are recognised in the grammar: statements, questions, commands, and explanations.

In describing the rules underlying the structure of utterances in English, GCE grants extensive coverage to all these aspects. In Table 1 some of the different components of the grammar which are discussed above are presented, together with explanations and examples from adult spoken syntax.

Quirk's tool of description (Quirk *et al.*, 1972) is, to date, the most systematic and definitive account of the grammar of English. Its application has been very broad in all spheres of language endeavour. It has also been most successfully applied by Crystal *et al.* (1976) as a descriptive framework for pathological language. The LARSP profile devised by these authors uses the terminology and structural distinctions suggested by Quirk *et al.* (1972). In rationalising the choice of Quirk's grammar, Crystal *et al.* (1976) made the following points:

> 1. That the Quirk method (unlike many other available methods of language analysis) is comprehensive and systematic, and that it accounts for all the spoken utterances of the individual, whether he be adult or child, his language normal or disordered.
>
> 2. That this grammar provides a uniform terminology and notation which, together with a clarity of descriptive apparatus, makes it easier for the practitioner to work with.
>
> 3. That the grammar, since it contains minimal theoretical exposition, is a tool which will remain relatively stable over time, and that it is therefore a measure enabling long-term/longitudinal investigations and comparisons of language.
>
> 4. That the grammar is empirically based, and further that it describes the rules of spoken as opposed to written syntax. It is thus a more realistic tool for the clinician dealing with the characterisation of language pathology.

	Name		Age		Sample date		Type	
A	Unanalysed				Problematic			
	1 Unintelligible		2 Symbolic Noise	3 Deviant	1 Incomplete		2 Ambiguous	3 Stereotypes

B	Responses			Normal Response					Abnormal		
			Repet-itions	Major			Red-uced	Full	Minor	Struc-tural	Ø	Prob-lems
	Stimulus type	Totals		Elliptical								
				1	2	3+						
		Questions										
		Others										
C	Spontaneous										
D	Reactions			General		Structural	Ø		Other		Problems

Stage I (0,9–1,6)	Minor		*Responses*			*Vocatives*		*Other*	*Problems*
		Comm.	Quest.		Statement				
	Major	'V'	'Q'	'V'		'N'	Other		Problems
Stage II (1,6–2,0)	Conn.		Clause				Phrase		Word
		VX	QX	SV	AX		DN	VV	-ing
				SO	VO		Adj N	V part	
				SC	VC		NN	Int X	pl
				Neg X	Other		PrN	Other	
Stage III (2,0–2,6)	X + S:NP		X + V:VP	X + C:NP		X + O:NP		X + A:AP	-ed
			Q X Y	SVC	VCA		D Adj N	Cop	-en
	V X Y			SVO	VOA		Adj Adj N	Aux^M_O	
	let X Y		VS (X)	SVA	VO$_d$O$_i$		Pr DN		3s
	do X Y			Neg X Y	Other		Pron^P_O	Other	
Stage IV (2,6–3,0)	X Y + S: NP		X Y + V:VP	X Y + C:NP	X Y + O:NP			X Y + A:AP	gen
	+ S		QVS	SVOA	AAXY		NP Pr NP	Neg V	n't
			QXY +	SVCA	Other		Pr D Adj N	Neg X	
	VXY +		VS(X+)	SVO$_d$O$_i$			c X	2 Aux	'cop
			tag	SVOC			Xc X	Other	
Stage V (3,0–3,6)	and	Coord.	Coord.	Coord.	1	1 +	Postmod. 1	1 +	'aux
	c	Other	Other	Subord. A	1	1 +	clause		-est
	s			S	C	O			
							Postmod. 1 +		-er
	Other			Comparative			phrase		-ly
		(+)				(−)			
Stage VI (3,6–4,6)		NP	VP	Clause	Conn.	Clause	Phrase		Word
						Element	NP	VP	N V
		Initiator	Complex	Passive	and	Ø	D Pr Pron^P	Aux^{M}Aux^{O}Cop	irreg
		Coord.		Complement.	c	⟷	DØ Pr Ø	⏜	
				how	s	Concord	D↕Pr↕	Ø	reg
				what					
	Other							Ambiguous	
Stage VII (4,6+)	*Discourse*				*Syntactic Comprehension*				
	A Connectivity		it						
	Comment Clause		there		*Style*				
	Emphatic Order		other						
	Total No. Sentences			Mean No. Sentences Per Turn			Mean Sentence Length		

Table 2: The LARSP Profile (Language Assessment Remediation Procedure). (From *Profiling Linguistic Ability*, by David Crystal. Edward Arnold, London, 1982)

The specific profile developed by Crystal and his associates (Crystal *et al.* 1976) will now be described in more detail. Crystal and his colleagues developed a profile, known as the LARSP profile, which divides the acquisition of syntax into seven stages. A revised version of the profile was published in 1982. These seven stages are discussed in detail in the succeeding chapter, but will be outlined here by way of an introduction, providing the reader with some orientation for an analysis of the LARSP profile which is reproduced in Table 2.

Briefly, the stages of language development in the normal child can be characterised as follows:

Stage I is the one-word stage and occurs between nine and eighteen months. The child uses single words to convey a variety of meanings – these words may resemble nouns or verbs, or may be social words such as 'hi' and 'hello'.

Stage II begins when the child starts putting words together. This generally occurs at eighteen months, and has been described as a period of linguistic 'explosion' because the child shows a rapid spurt in the development of his linguistic ability. At this stage we may note the combination of elements such as subject and verb (Mommy go), or simply the beginnings of small phrases, with, for example, the use of determiners and adjectives before a noun (the book, big hat), and the use of adverbs and prepositions. Many would argue that to talk of syntax alone at this stage is to hold a very restricted view of child language. It is imperative in this context that we remember both the semantic and pragmatic levels of language. However, syntax may be viewed as the building blocks of language, without which the child is very restricted in his capacity to convey a range of meanings.

Stage III starts at about the age of two, and occurs when the child begins to string together three elements or to use three-word phrases. Some examples of Stage III utterances are:

>   Man eat dinner.
>   The bicycle moves quickly.

At this stage the child starts to develop pronouns as well as the auxiliary verb. These are both very important areas of concern for the language teacher as we often note that these areas are under-developed in language disabled children.

Stage IV involves further development of many of these aspects of language, and the child is now using full sentences. Some examples of the utterances a child uses at this stage are:

>   Mommy gave the ball to me.
>   Yesterday I ate lunch.

Stage V occurs at about three years of age, when the child begins to join sentences together either by means of co-ordinators or subordinators. This stage represents an important hurdle for the language-impaired child, and in therapy we often find that a child will become stuck at Stage IV and have great difficulty in learning to combine sentences. We also note at this stage the development of post-modification, which is the elaboration of the noun phrase and the use of relative sentences. An example of an utterance which occurs in the normal child at this stage is:

>   The ball Mommy gave me got lost and I cannot find it.

Stage VI begins by the age of four. During this stage we are more impressed by the fact that the child has language that is similar to his adult models, than by the differences between the child's language and adult language. There are still some immaturities that may remain in the child's speech, for example the incorrect use of pronouns, but by and large there is an increased complexity in areas such as the verb phrase.

Stage VII involves a further development of grammar. The child gains control of his language, and his use of discourse becomes more sophisticated – he now strings sentences together into paragraphs. He is able to tell a story about a sequence of events, and is able to link his sentences using stylistic and cohesive grammatical and lexical devices.

In a short period of time then, the normal child moves from the one-word level to a level of syntax equivalent to that of the adult. There are many theories as to how this happens, and many controversies as to what is required to make it happen.

Language development becomes the therapist's concern when it fails to occur. There are many different reasons for language delay, some of which may be related to constitutional factors such as hearing loss, brain damage, or retardation; and some of which are environmental, for example institutionalisation, deprivation, or poor speech models. The single greatest cause of language delay is unknown; the interactive nature of causes is on the other hand very well documented. We assume that, as far as possible, the diagnostician will try to establish causal factors, and (where relevant) will attempt to eliminate and reduce those factors which continue to impair language development. The way in which therapists work on language is different with different cases, but the sequence in which we progress is essentially identical – that is, we plan to bring the child to the point of language development which is appropriate for his mental age. For example if we note that a four-year-old child is using only two-word sentences, we will quickly be able to conclude that he has a language delay. Other language problems may be more subtle though, and will require a detailed diagnosis. This is where LARSP helps. If we undertake a LARSP analysis: we are able to establish exactly where the child is in relation to his age group; we can see at a glance his areas of strength and weakness; and we can ascertain the range of structures he uses at clause, phrase and word levels.

In addition, the LARSP profile gives us information as to what proportion of the language sample is unanalysable (for example, how many utterances are unintelligible or deviant), as well as giving us information about how the child responds to input. It will also produce information about the nature of the language that the child's interactive partner is using; for example, it will reveal both the proportion of questions in the interaction, and how the partner reacts to the utterances of the child (Section D on the LARSP profile). All this information becomes important when we are diagnosing and planning the therapy programme.

A word of caution may be appropriate here. It takes time to learn how to do LARSP, to which many of our undergraduate speech-therapy students can attest. No one can expect to learn this method without the aid and benefit of the original book and, preferably, a workshop on its application. Though the analysis is not difficult it does require a set of skills which have to be learnt. An inaccurate analysis is of less use than the paper on which it is written. Though this book will provide a detailed consideration of the stages of LARSP and how to work on them in therapy, it does not directly address the technique of sample analysis. If the language therapist or teacher is unfamiliar with this method, we suggest that they enlist the aid of someone who can help them to accurately characterise the child's position on the profile. Thereafter, with the help of this book, the therapy programme can commence once the areas of deficiency have been identified.

In planning the therapy programme one looks at where the child is on the profile, and where he should be in terms of his age and the correlating stage of language development. The therapy process is aimed at taking the child down the profile in as systematic a way as possible, keeping a balance between clause, phrase and word levels. Thus, for example, if a four-year-old is at Stage II, you will need to consolidate his language in this stage by teaching a variety of two-element utterances. Then you will have to teach him structures that appear in Stage III, before moving to the stage that he should have achieved. This sounds self-evident, but it contrasts with many alternative therapy programmes which may be non-developmental, or which may focus on vocabulary or one component of syntax without paying

SCORE	INDEFINITE PRONOUNS OR NOUN MODIFIERS	PERSONAL PRONOUNS	MAIN VERBS	SECONDARY VERBS
1	it, this, that	1st and 2nd person: I, me, my, mine, you, your(s)	A. Uninflected Verb: I *see* you. B. copula, is or 's: *It's* red. C. is + verb + ing: He *is coming*	
2		3rd person: he, him, his, she, her, hers	A. -s and -ed: *plays, played* B. irregular past: *ate, saw* C. Copula: *am, are, was, were* D. Auxiliary: *am, are, was, were*	Five early-developing infinitives: I wan*na see* (want *to see*) I'm gon*na see* (going *to see*) I got*ta see* (got *to see*) Lem*me* [*to*] *see* (let me [*to*] *see*) Let's [to] play (let [us *to*] *play*)
3	A. no, some, more, all, lot(s), one(s), two (etc.), other(s), another B. something, somebody, someone	A. Plurals: we, us, our(s), they, them, their B. these, those		Non-complementing infinitives: I stopped *to play*. I'm afraid *to look*. It's hard *to do* that.
4	nothing, nobody, none, no one		A. can, will, may + verb: *may go* B. Obligatory do + verb: *don't go* C. Emphatic do + verb: I *do see*.	Participle, present or past: I see a boy *running*. I found the toy *broken*.
5		Reflexives: myself, yourself, himself, herself, itself, themselves		A. Early infinitival complements with differing subjects in kernels: I want you *to come*. Let him [*to*] *see*. B. Later infinitival complements: I had *to go*. I told him *to go*. I tried *to go*. He ought *to go*. C. Obligatory deletions: Make it [*to*] *go* I'd better [*to*] *go* D. Infinitive with wh-word: I know what *to get*. I know how *to do it*.

Table 3: Developmental Sentence Analysis (From Laura Lee, *Developmental Sentence Analysis: A Grammatical Procedure for Speech and Language Clinicians.* Northwestern University Press, Evanston, 1974)

| NEGATIVES | CONJUNCTIONS | QUESTIONS ||
		INTERROGATIVE REVERSALS	WH-QUESTIONS
it, this, that + copula or auxiliary is, 's, + not: 　it's *not* mine. 　This is *not* a dog. 　That is *not* moving.		Reversal of copula: *Is*n't *it* red? *Were they* there?	
			A. who, what, what + noun: 　*Who* am I? *What* is he eating? *What book* are you reading? B. where, how many, how much, what ... do, what ... for 　*Where* did it go? 　*How much* do you want? 　*What* is he *doing*? 　*What* is the hammer *for*?
	and		
can't, don't		Reversal of auxiliary be: 　*Is he* coming? 　*Is*n't *he* coming? 　*Was he* going? 　*Was*n't *he* going?	
isn't, won't	A. but B. so, and so, so that C. or, if		when, how, how + adjective 　*When* shall I come? 　*How* do you do it? 　*How big* is it?

17

SCORE	INDEFINITE PRONOUNS OR NOUN MODIFIERS	PERSONAL PRONOUNS	MAIN VERBS	SECONDARY VERBS
6		A. Wh-pronouns: who, which, whose, whom, what, that, how many, how much I know *who* came. That's *what* I said. B. Wh-word + infinitive: I know *what* to do. I know *who(m)* to take.	A. Could, would, should, might + verb: *might come*, *could be* B. Obligatory does, did + verb C. emphatic does, did + verb	
7	A. any, anything, anybody, anyone B. every, everything, everybody, everyone C. both, few, many, each, several, most, least, much, next, first, last, second (etc.)	(his) own, one, oneself, whichever, whoever, whatever Take *whatever* you like	A. Passive with *get*, any tense Passive with *be*, any tense B. must, shall + verb: *must come* C. have + verb + en: *I've eaten* D. have got: *I've got* it	Passive infinitival complement: With *get*: I have *to get dressed*. I don't want *to get hurt*. With *be*: I want *to be pulled*. It's going *to be locked*.
8			A. have been + verb + ing had been + verb + ing B. modal + have + verb + en: *may have eaten* C. modal + be + verb + ing: *could be playing* D. Other auxiliary combinations: *should have been sleeping*	Gerund: *Swinging* is fun. I like *fishing*. He started *laughing*.

Table 3 (continued): Developmental Sentence Analysis

| NEGATIVES | CONJUNCTIONS | QUESTIONS ||
		INTERROGATIVE REVERSALS	WH-QUESTIONS
	because	A. Obligatory do, does, did: *Do they* run? *Does it* bite? *Did*n't *it* hurt? B. Reversal of modal: *Can you* play? *Wo*n't *it* hurt? *Shall* I sit down? C. Tag question: It's fun, *isn't it?* It isn't fun, *is it?*	
All other negatives: A. Uncontracted negatives: I can *not* go. He has *not* gone. B. Pronoun-auxiliary or pronoun-copula contraction: I'm *not* coming. He's *not* here. C. Auxiliary-negative or copula-negative contraction: He was*n't* going. He has*n't* been seen. It could*n't* be mine. They are*n't* big.			why, what if, how come, how about + gerund *Why* are you crying? *What if* I won't do it? *How come* he is crying? *How about* coming with me?
	A. where, when, how, while, whether (or not), till, until, unless, since, before, after, for, as, as + adjective + as, as if, like, that, than I know *where* you are. Don't come *till* I call. B. Obligatory deletions: I run faster *than* you [run]. I'm *as big as* a man [is big]. It looks *like* a dog [looks]. C. Elliptical deletions (score 0): That's *why* [I took it]. I know *how* [I can do it]. D. Wh-words + infinitive: I know *how* to do it. I know *where* to go.	A. Reversal of auxiliary have: *Has he* seen you? B. Reversal with two or three auxiliaries: *Has he been* eating? *Could*n't *he have* waited? *Could he have been* crying? *Would*n't *he have been* going?	whose, which, which + noun *Whose* car is that? *Which book* do you want?

attention to the variety of structures that are necessary before the successive stage of language can be reached.

At this point it might be useful to indicate the common problem areas which are found in the language-impaired child, areas to which the clinician should be particularly alerted. One of these areas, as we have already mentioned, is the **auxiliary**. Many language-impaired children show difficulties in using any elaborated verb structure, and will rely heavily on main verbs (the boy swims), or on the simple copula or verb to be. The auxiliary is however a prerequisite for the development of some other important grammatical structures. For example the development of grammatically correct yes/no questions relies on the use of (and inversion of) the auxiliary. Similarly the marking of a negative verb within the sentence requires the use of an auxiliary.

Another danger area is the **pronoun**, particularly the personal pronoun. The language-impaired child may well have a restricted and inaccurate use of pronouns. Other problems occur (as discussed) at the stage of **sentence recursion**, where the child may well experience problems joining the sentences which he has learned.

Laura Lee in her development of a method of syntax analysis known as *Developmental Sentence Analysis*, actually specified eight grammatical areas which are frequently problematic for the language-impaired child and which may require specific attention. These are portrayed in Table 3, where each of these structures is illustrated and the stages of development in the normal child are represented. Although in Lee's case there are no ages attached to stages, this particular order of acquisition seems to be inviolate. We have found that Lee's approach to grammatical development serves as a direct complement to the LARSP approach discussed above. In a sense Lee's outline of the sequence of acquisition of the various structures acts as a 'fine tune' for the general area identified on the LARSP. For example through LARSP you may establish that the pronoun is inadequate. You can then refer to the Lee chart in order to see which pronouns appear first and which presuppose the development of others.

In Table 3, her developmental chart for eight grammatical categories is presented. Those interested in how Lee developed her scoring method should refer to her *Developmental Sentence Analysis* (1974). There is also a book entitled *Normal Language Development* by Trantham and Peterson (1972), which charts the longitudinal language development of a group of normal children and of one language-impaired child. This book uses Lee's categories, something that the reader might find useful.

How does this help you? In the following chapters you will see how we combine both these methods. LARSP is used as the primary method, and we will work through each stage showing what is acquired and how to teach each structure. The Lee approach will be incorporated into this method, and will guide you as to the sequence of teaching certain specific structures which are under scrutiny. We have found Lee's approach particularly useful for teaching aspects of the verb. Other categories given individual attention are pronouns, conjunctions and questions. We have added three more categories which we feel are of relevance, namely prepositions, articles, adjectives and adverbs.

The final point to remember about assessment is that it should be repeated at regular intervals throughout the process of therapy. Crystal actually suggests that language should be assessed every month. It is only through repeated reassessment that we are able to see the effectiveness of our therapy in terms of its rate, its pace and its content. It also delineates the path of further therapy.

In summary the **stages of assessment** are:

The collection of a representative language sample.

The transcription of the sample.

The analysis of the sample.

The interpretation of the analysis.

The delineation of therapy aims.

The monthly resampling of the child's language.

Again, we both receive pleas from those with large caseloads and busy schedules about the lengthy process of the transcription, analysis and interpretation which is involved in assessment. We tend to be unsympathetic to such complaints. The time spent in assessment is entirely justified if it enables the delineation of clear and unambiguous therapy goals. The therapist is accountable, and all work should be goal-directed. LARSP enables you to establish the goal, and also provides you with the steps with which to achieve it. In our opinion, no standardised test does this adequately.

To illustrate this process we have included a brief extract from the language sample of a 4.6 year old language-impaired child, and the LARSP profile resulting from the analysis of a fifteen-minute language sample offered by Crystal (1982, pp. 46-48.)

T	have you ˈgot one like thát /	*referring to carpet*
P	nò/	
T	nòt like ˈthat/	
	ˈwhat ˈcolour's yóurs/	
P	me – ˈme ain't gòt cárpets/	
T	you ˈhaven't got cărpets/	
	ˈwhat dò you have/	
P	ˈjust	
T	this/	
	this sort of thíng/	*referring to a bathroom mat*
P	yēah/	
T	well this is a sort of cárpet/ isn't it/	
P	nò/	
	lòok/	
T	oh it's beaùtifully ˈsoft/ isn't it/	
P	thàt/ can ˈgo upstàirs/	
T	yès/	
	thàt's trúe/	
P	(1 *syll*) dòwnstairs thére/	
T	wêll/	
P	ˈwhat's thàt/	
T	ˈwhat do you think it ˈis/	
P	oh is –	
	is ˈthat a mìrror/ isn't it/	
T	it isn't a mírror/beˈcause you ˈcan't sèe yourˈself/ –	
	it's a ˈsort of cùpboard/.	
	I ˈthink ˈthat one ˈgoes aˈgainst the wàll/–	
	can you ˈput it aˈgainst the wáll ˈsomewhere/ – –	
P	(5 *sylls*)	
T	ˈwill it ŏpen/	
P	nò/	
T	yès it wíll/	
	ˈthat's grèat/	
P	Ì can – Ì can pút/ – tòys in thére/	
T	if we hàd any tóys/ –	
	but we ˈdon't ˈseem to hàve any ˈtoys in thís ˈhouse/ – –	
	ˈwhat ˈtoys have yòu got/	
	ˈwhat's your bèst ˈtoy/	
P	ràcing ˈcar/	
T	a ràcing ˈcar/	
P	yèah/	
T	and ˈdoes it have a tràck to gó on/	
P	nó/	

Name: Shane P.   Age: 4;6   Sample date: 25·11·80   Type: Free play toys (15 mins)

A Unanalysed
1 Unintelligible 9   2 Symbolic Noise   3 Deviant

Problematic
1 Incomplete 4   2 Ambiguous   3 Stereotypes 7

B Responses

Stimulus type	Totals	Repetitions	Elliptical 1	Elliptical 2	Elliptical 3+	Reduced	Full	Minor	Structural	Ø	Problems
Questions	66 / 59		15	4	2		2	32	4	5	
Others	44 / 36	1	8				12	14	2		

C Spontaneous 39
7   6   5   11   10

D Reactions 95
General 30 | Structural 21 | Ø 43 | Other 1 | Problems

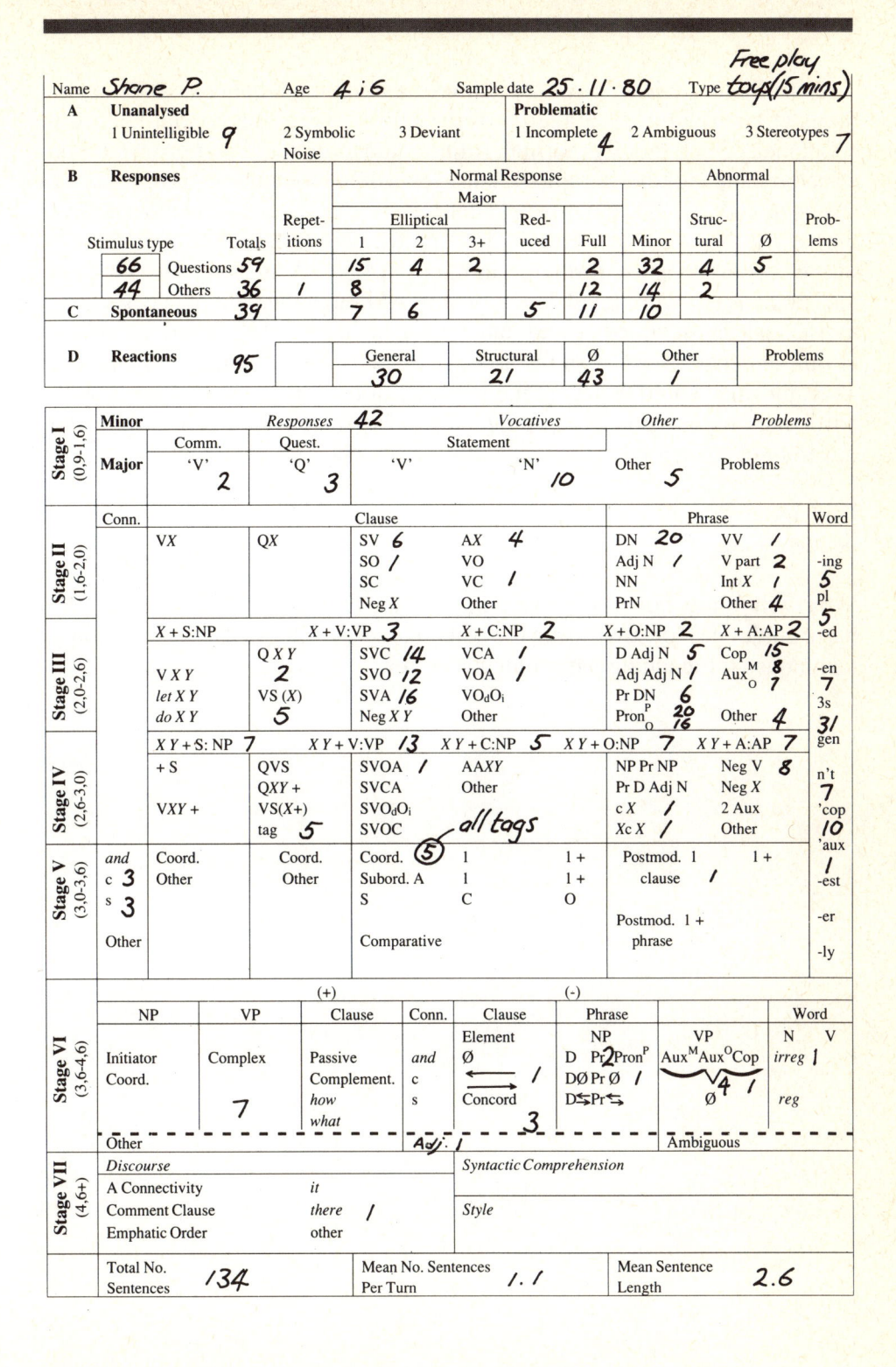

Stage I (0.9–1.6)
Minor   Responses 42   Vocatives   Other   Problems
Major — Comm. 'V' 2 | Quest. 'Q' 3 | Statement 'V' — 'N' 10 | Other 5 | Problems

Stage II (1.6–2.0)
Conn. | Clause: VX | QX | SV 6 | AX 4 | Phrase: DN 20 | VV 1 | Word: -ing 5
SO 1 | VO | Adj N 1 | V part 2 | pl 5
SC | VC 1 | NN | Int X 1
Neg X | Other | PrN | Other 4

Stage III (2.0–2.6)
X+S:NP | X+V:VP 3 | X+C:NP 2 | X+O:NP 2 | X+A:AP | -ed
VXY | QXY | SVC 14 | VCA 1 | D Adj N 5 | Cop 15 | -en
let XY | VS(X) | SVO 12 | VOA 1 | Adj Adj N 1 | Aux^M 8 / ^{O} 7
do XY | 5 | SVA 16 | VO$_d$O$_i$ | Pr DN 6 | | 3s
 | | Neg XY | Other | Pron^P 20 / ^{O} 16 | Other 4 | gen 31

Stage IV (2.6–3.0)
XY+S:NP 7 | XY+V:VP 13 | XY+C:NP 5 | XY+O:NP 7 | XY+A:AP 7
+S | QVS | SVOA 1 | AAXY | NP Pr NP | Neg V 8 | n't 7
 | QXY+ | SVCA | Other | Pr D Adj N | Neg X | 'cop 10
VXY+ | VS(X+) | SVO$_d$O$_i$ | | cX 1 | 2 Aux | 'aux 1
 | tag 5 | SVOC 5 — all tags | | Xc X 1 | Other

Stage V (3.0–3.6)
and c 3 | Coord. | Coord. | Coord. 5 | 1 | 1+ | Postmod. 1 | 1+ | -est
s 3 | Other | Other | Subord. A | 1 | 1+ | clause 1 | | -er
 | | | S | C | O | Postmod. 1+ phrase | | -ly
Other | | | Comparative | | | | |

Stage VI (3.6–4.6)
(+) NP | VP | Clause | Conn. | (-) Clause | Phrase | | Word
Initiator | Complex | Passive | and | Element Ø | NP: D Pr 2 Pron^P | VP: Aux^M Aux^O Cop | N V
Coord. | | Complement. | c | ↔ 1 | DØ Pr Ø 1 | √ 4 1 | irreg 1
 | 7 | how | s | Concord 3 | D⇌Pr⇌ | Ø | reg
Other | | what | | Adj. 1 | | Ambiguous |

Stage VII (4.6+)
Discourse
A Connectivity | it
Comment Clause | there 1 | Syntactic Comprehension
Emphatic Order | other | Style

Total No. Sentences: 134   Mean No. Sentences Per Turn: 1.1   Mean Sentence Length: 2.6

Table 4: LARSP profile demonstrating language delay

23

The profile in Table 4 shows a picture of grammatical delay with the stage focus at approximately Stage III of the profile. It reveals a relatively low spontaneity, but largely normal (minor and elliptical) responses to the structured input of the therapist. Clause level development seems reasonably strong up to Stage III, and most elements show expansion. At a phrasal level the patient shows use of the auxiliary verb, which is reflected in the inversion of the verb in question form and in the use of Neg V at Stage IV. There is also evidence of word level development. Although the patient is beginning to use basic conjunctions ('and' and 'cos'), he has not developed the ability to link sentences because of the absence of clause development at Stage IV. Therapy aims would therefore include attention to Stage IV structures, with particular emphasis on developing subject expansions and verb forms, and developing sequential skills to encourage sentence combination.

With monthly reassessment, aims will change and different priorities might be identified.

What will follow now is a consideration of the therapeutic context and some basic guidelines for structuring the language session, as well as some therapy techniques for teaching particular structures.

2. Planning a Session

Play is the medium through which all language programmes should be delivered. Activities must be intriguing, joyous and playful. According to Gillham (1979), there are three fundamentals in the organisation of teaching, namely:

> 1. A good range of teaching materials and flexibility in using several ways to teach the same thing.
>
> 2. 'Formal' teaching – regular and structured teaching sessions.
>
> 3. 'Informal' teaching – this applies to naturally occurring events and situations. Apart from taking the opportunity to introduce these situations in therapy, you must have the skill to guide the family to incorporate specific language structures into everyday events in the home.

Children respond well to routine and control. Doing the same things, at the same time, in the same place, either in the clinic/school or at home, is helpful (Courtman-Davies 1979).

In your clinic or classroom, particularly when handling the young child, keep the toys you intend using out of sight and reach until you are ready to introduce them. This prevents distraction and enables the child to concentrate on one activity at a time. Children often have a short attention span, so carry out each activity just as long as the interest-level is held, and then move on to something else (Crawford 1979).

Be prepared to change in the face of changing circumstances. This refers to the need to monitor both the child's response, and his abilities to master the task at hand. For example, you may want to teach the plural auxiliary+ - **ing:**

> The boy and the girl are walking.

However, you ascertain during your lesson that the child has not mastered the singular auxiliary **is**, which precedes the plural. You need to backtrack and contrast **is** and **are**.

It is helpful to regard each session as a miniature research project. You hypothesise that the child will have a certain level of competence – let us say Stage IV (LARSP).

Your aim may be to teach the structure **SVOA**, with expansion of **A:AP**.

Target:
Robyn, put the banana/apple in the basket/box.

Material:
A banana; an apple; a box; a basket.

Activity:
Having identified each object, you devise a game to use the target structure.

Result:
Although the child comprehends the structure, he is unable to include both the verb and the preposition in this complex utterance:
The banana in the basket.
or
Robyn, put the banana basket.

Conclusion:

The structure is too advanced for his expressive competence. Separate it into its parts, and re-drill the adverbial phrase A:AP; then combine it with the verb and object, and finally add a subject to the clause.

Always design your activity to ensure that the child will be encouraged to generate the target in a variety of contexts. Firstly, make sure that he is familiar with each of the items or concepts you have selected to make up the target utterance. Do this by asking him to choose the relevant items named from the objects of your choice, and to perform actions for the verbs you name.

Now devise your activity, varying one element at a time.

Target:

SVO$_d$O$_i$ (LARSP Stage IV) Subject Verb

Direct Object Indirect Object.

Mommy/Daddy give(s) (a) ball/banana to (the) girl/boy.

Activity 1:

VO$_d$O$_i$
Give the ball to the girl.

Materials:
A ball; a girl model.

Activity:
Instruct the child:
'Give the ball to the girl!'

Reverse roles, allowing the child to instruct you.

Activity 2:

SVO$_d$O$_i$
Mommy, give (the) ball to (the) girl.

Materials:
A ball, a mommy and girl models.

Activity:
Instruct the mommy model:
'Mommy, give the ball to the girl!'

Allow the child to issue the instruction.

Activity 3:
SVO$_d$O$_i$ varying the Indirect Object.
Mommy, give (a) ball to (the) boy/girl.

Materials:
Model mommy, girl and boy dolls; two balls.

Activity:
Instruct the Mommy doll:
'Mommy, give a ball to the boy!'
'Mommy, give a ball to the girl!'

Let the child activate the models while issuing instructions.

Activity 4:
SVO$_d$O$_i$ varying both the Subject and the Indirect Object.
Mommy/Daddy, give the ball to the boy/girl.

Materials:
Model doll family, two balls.

Activity:
Instruct the family members to act, varying the characters appropriately:
'Mommy, give a ball to the boy!
'Daddy, give a ball to the girl!'
Finally, introduce a variable for the direct object – banana/ball.
Any number of variables may be introduced in this manner.

Hypothesis:

Having assessed the child's language competence, you hypothesise as to his stage of receptive and expressive development.

> **Example:**
> Ralph is at stage IV (LARSP).
>
> **Aim:**
> Select a relevant Stage IV structure and aim to teach it:
>
> QVS – with expansion of one element.

Methodology

Think of several examples of your selected structure:

Where's (the) big red ball?	QVS – S:NP
	NP: Adj Adj N
Who wants this car?	QVS – S:NP
	NP: Det N
What are you doing?	QVS – V:VP
	VP: Aux + - ing

In what contexts are these applicable?

> 'Where's the big red ball?'
> The ball will not be in view of the questioner. There must be a selection of balls – the request is for a specific one – it's red and not blue, it's big and not small.

> 'Who want(s) this car?'
> There are several cars to choose from and several people being questioned.

> 'What are you doing?'
> The questioner is unable to see the person addressed, or is unfamiliar with the activity in progress.

Equipment:

Do you have the necessary items named in the target utterances? If not, can you illustrate them or substitute other available items?

Method:

Vary one element at a time, gradually increasing the complexity.

Target:

Where's (the) big red ball?

Equipment:

A big red ball; a small red ball; a big blue ball; a small blue ball.

Activity:

1. QVS (no expansion)

Select one ball only. The child hides it.
You ask:
'Where's the ball?'
He may say:
'Under the table.'
He may point to the hiding place, or assist you to hunt for it.
Now reverse roles so that he uses the target utterance.

2. QVS (S:NP = (Det) Adj N)

Repeat the activity, this time hiding a red ball and a blue ball in two different locations. The target is now:

Where's (the) red ball? Where's (the) blue ball?

> ### 3. QVS (S: (Det) Adj Adj N)
> Repeat the activity, hiding four balls – a big red ball, a small red ball, a big blue ball and a small blue ball.
>
> **Target:**
> Where's (the) big red ball?
>
> When the child has retrieved all four balls by using the target appropriately, and has correctly requested you to do so too, praise him for his efforts.

Results:

During the activity you will be noting responses and problems. In this case, Ralph was able to complete steps 1 and 2 satisfactorily, but became confused at stage 3 although you had worked on the phrase **Adj Adj N** in isolation during your last session.

Conclusion:

Ralph is not yet able to extend a noun phrase to three elements when embedding it in a three-element clause. You need to revise **Adj Adj N**, and to embed it in varied structures.

3. The Importance of Reception

Parents have successfully been teaching their children to talk for centuries, and yet researchers into child language have only recently begun to study parent–infant communication. We are now borrowing some of the techniques used by parents in order to remediate language-delayed and language-deviant children.

Researchers (Snow and Ferguson 1977; Phillips 1973; Muma 1978; De Maio 1983) have described some of the characteristics of caretakers' communication with their children, and we would do well to emulate them.

We, as therapists, adopt De Maio's maxim that 'Language must be taught through the child's activity, in the context of communication, and through social interaction, which is a critical component in the language-learning process.'

Adult/child interaction begins in the neo-natal period and is mutual. Therefore the sooner remediation begins, and parents are assisted to maintain appropriate communication strategies with their children, the more effective intervention will be. Adults modify their speech to accommodate the child's level of communicative competence. Some of these modifications may include: a slower rate of speaking; higher pitch; and even changes in syntactic form such as the use of redundancies, for example, 'You know the little white dog – the dog with the white fur. Well, he came in wagging his little white tail.' Crystal *et al.* (1976) advocate using language one level more advanced than the child's own competence when conversing with him.

This will enable the child both to decode the message and to master more complex structures. If a child has a lowered level of competence, the maxim 'Talk, talk, talk!' is of dubious value. Thus if the child has no expressive competence, it may be necessary to speak to him in single words. These may be effectively varied by altering suprasegmental features in order to represent questions, commands or statements:

>'Ball?' ('Where's the ball?');

>'Ball!' ('There's the ball!').

Speaking in 'full sentences', which has been advocated by some remediators, makes little sense if the child is unable to decode a complex message (see Book Two, The First Lexicon). Be sure to use a conversational approach, talking about things of the moment.

Formal and outdated structures should be avoided, and colloquial language forms most familiar to the child should be used. Crystal *et al.* (1976) state that even the written form must conform to the spoken word. 'Please may I have...' should be replaced by 'Can I have...?' or 'Please give me...'. 'It is a...' becomes 'It's a...', and 'Do not...' becomes 'Don't!'.

(These colloquial forms may be more difficult for the hearing-impaired child to perceive, but the use of manual coding will provide an added cue.)

It is primarily important to allow the young child an opportunity to set the topic of conversation whenever possible, and for the adult to do most of the back-chanelling. For example:

>   Child: 'Truck!'

>   Adult: 'A big truck!'

When the child points to an object, he is introducing a topic even if he says or signs nothing, and this should become the focus of interest for the moment. Our aim is to model or expand for the child, and our response should in turn stimulate his further attempts to communicate.

Figure 1: The Cultural Context.

4. Creating Relevance and Context

Cognition is the foundation upon which language is built. 'When the goal is teaching language, the result is mimicry. When the goal is stimulating thought, the result is language' (Eccarius 1979).

The activity designed by the therapist must be in accord with the child's world, and must be applicable to varied communicative contexts. One of our students, in a desperate attempt to use her available equipment to teach the preposition **under**, manipulated the models to demonstrate:

'The boy is under the cow – the cow is under the boy'!

Using syntactic forms in inappropriate contexts is not conducive to communication!

Many school programmes introduce the present continuous tense as the first verb form which the child is expected to learn. However when they first begin to speak, children use uninflected verbs, and the present continuous is appropriate only for descriptive narratives such as 'The sun is shining and the birds are singing' (Sinoff 1985).

Before the child learns a linguistic form, he must understand the concept which underlies the form. The colour lexicon is a good example. Studies have shown that until a child is able to classify objects by colour, as opposed to form or use, he will not learn colour names. Test this out by giving the child selected objects: a blue ball, plane, car and shoe; a red ball, plane, car and shoe; and a yellow ball, plane, car and shoe. Demonstrate that you want him to match these according to colour, and see if he is capable of doing so by ignoring the other variables.

Context

The context in which language takes place has been described by Halliday (1973) as 'who does what, where, when, why and how'. There are thus several components to context which should be taken into account when teaching. These include the situational context, the linguistic context and the listener context.

The situational context

1. Make sure that your activity is age appropriate and that the materials you select will therefore provide an appropriate stimulus. For example, children under two years of age are likely to name a model doll 'baba', so the use of a model doll family before the age of three will not serve to teach family names.

2. Take cognisance of the cultural milieu in which the child is raised. Your selection of an initial lexicon will depend upon the objects and activities in the child's home environment. 'Refrigerator' and 'television' may be relevant for a city dweller, but we selected 'hoe' and 'pot' for rural Ciskeians. Even your pictorial representations must be familiar to the child – our pot was of the large, black three-legged variety.

3. The child must at all times be aware of what the communicative interaction is about. For example, he must know the target or speech event if you aim to teach the wh-question 'where?'. Allow him to play the role of both questioner and respondent, hiding and seeking an object, so that the word 'where' takes on real significance.

The intentional context

A variety of intentional contexts must be provided, and may include requests for objects (instrumental); and for action (regulatory); and comments on actions (personal). Examples of activities illustrating these intentions may be seen in our suggested activities.

The linguistic context

Language is a set of sentences which are woven together through their underlying frame, through congruence with the ongoing situation, and through the shared knowledge held by the speaker and listener. In addition, '... sentences are tied together linguistically' (Lund and Duchan 1983, p. 56).

Anaphora is one device used to tie sentences together when something which has previously been identified is referred to at a later stage in a narrative. '**The lady** went to the shop. **She** bought some fruit, and then **she** went home.' Therefore it is very important when teaching linguistic forms such as pronouns to effect 'carry-over' by teaching the child the art of story-telling (see Book Two: The Child's Own Narration).

The listener context

This refers to the speaker's ability to consider the listener's perspective. Again, this is best taught by allowing the child to reverse roles so that he can comprehend the perspective of both the sender and receiver of the message. For example if two toys – a car and a ball – have been hidden, asking the child 'Where is it?' is not sufficient information for the listener to identify the toy requested, and the child will discover this in context.

The conversational context

All language should be taught in a meaningful, interactive context. Reciting structures by rote must be avoided at all costs, however tempting this might be in terms of drilling new words or syntax. Conversational strategies such as turn-taking, introducing a new topic, and the polite forms relevant to the situation will only be acquired in context.

5. Motivation

Merely 'learning' words and grammatical structures in the classroom or clinic gives no guarantee of their effective use in daily communicative contexts. A need must be created for using newly acquired language as a tool to manipulate the world. This need is the most effective motivation for vocalising, verbalising or signing. When the child realises that a toy is activated by his own command 'Go', or that he gets that apple when he asks for it, then language has become functional for him. Carry-over from the clinic to the social milieu is therefore essential. At the end of every session our pre-schoolers are rewarded with a sweet. They usually point to the cupboard and babble unintelligibly. The therapist adopts a puzzled expression, walks to the cupboard door, and stands immobile. She responds to nothing short of an attempt to approximate the word 'sweet' (although she may have to model in a questioning tone: 'Sweet?'). An adequate attempt is immediately rewarded, but the demand progresses to 'Want sweet', 'I want a sweet', and finally the cherry on the top, 'Please'. This complexity will depend on the stage of language development.

The family must be taught to use this process at home, with due consideration to the fact that it will not be possible, practical, or wise to do so on every occasion that the child attempts to communicate.

Sometimes it is necessary to resort to tokens as a reward for speaking or responding to communication. In the early stages of single-word differentiation, the correct identification of named objects or pictures may be rewarded by allowing the child to thread another bead on his necklace, or place another block on his tower.

The edible reward – a Smartie or raisin – is the 'bottom of the rung', but sometimes it is an unavoidable necessity, especially when faced with the need to drill, as for example with the Ling phonetic exercises (1976). However it should not be necessary to resort to this form of motivation in pragmatic language tasks as a reward will be inherent in the activity. For example, by asking for the 'red car' in a game to teach colour names, the child is given the car. If he says 'car', the adult looks puzzled and uses the forced alternative technique in order to elicit an adequate response: 'The red car or the yellow car?'. Remember to ensure that your goals are clear to the child himself (Courtman Davies 1979).

Be sure to work with equipment and activities that are age-appropriate and interesting to the child. It is very easy to teach 'fast and slowly' by using model cars with a four-year-old boy! One of our students devised a war game using model soldiers, tanks and planes, in order to teach adjectives to an eleven-year-old deaf boy.

Never repeat an activity over and over again. Show the child in tangible form that there is a limit. For example, in an activity to teach the pronouns **me** and **you**, counters may be shared between therapist/teacher and child: 'One for me – one for you'. Place a limited number of counters between you, and do not replenish the store when they have all been shared out.

6. Techniques

Muma (1978) lists several of the basic techniques with which most readers may be familiar.

Expansion

This occurs when the child's utterance is expanded into the correct grammatical form.

>Child: 'Mommy car.'
>Adult: 'Yes, Mommy's going in the car.'

It is an effective way to teach language. Adding something to the words the child has just produced confirms that his response is appropriate, and takes him slightly beyond the response, modelling extra grammatical forms just when he is most attentive.

However some researchers argue that expansions may simply be functioning as a back-channeling device to confirm the adult's understanding of an utterance (Crystal *et al.* 1976).

Simple expatiation

The adult makes comments about the child's utterance, but keeps these relevant to the utterance:

>Child: 'Mommy, look doggie!'
>Adult: 'Yes, that's a big doggie.'

As the child sets the topic, the adult responds relevantly, encouraging continued communicative exchange. So often we tend to make irrelevant comments, blocking any further discourse. The child says, 'Car go!' and we respond, 'What colour is the car?'.

Alternative model

When we enquire about the meaning or logic of an utterance, we encourage the child to think of alternative ways to express his ideas.

>Child: 'I've got a plaster.'
>Adult: 'How did you hurt yourself?'

Asking relevant questions of children (following their statements), is far more effective than trying to initiate conversation by asking questions (Kretschmer and Kretschmer 1978). How often do we hear desperate students at our out-patients' clinic attempting to elicit a language sample by asking a child questions such as, 'What did you do at school today?', 'What's the name of your teacher?'. Crystal *et al.*(1976) claim that some questions are easier to answer than others. It is easier to answer a yes/no question than a wh-question, since the latter requires a lengthier reply. The most difficult question to answer is a general one, for example, 'What's happening in this picture?'. It is not helpful in teaching language to ask this type of question, as it offers no syntactic leads.

Discourse with a language-disabled child needs to be planned according to the structures to be elicited. Asking, 'What are the children doing?' will elicit the morphological marker -ing ('jumping'). Demanding the full clause, 'The children are jumping', as a response is not in accord with discourse in context (see Forced Alternative, below).

Teaching the question form itself plays a very important part in language teaching (see the section on Questions in Book 3).

Over and above the devices used in regular adult–child discourse, there are techniques devised for developing and correcting language. The more successful of these do not violate conversational rules. Many, although ingenious, are used inappropriately with the very young child, serving only to drill meaningless grammatical forms which are unlikely to be used spontaneously.

Imitation – or 'Say what I say'

Most writers acknowledge that imitation tasks *per se* are of limited value. Only when the child assumes an active role by deducing rules from the language which has been modelled by the adult, will the child internalise and generate language. Kretschmer and Kretschmer (1978) give an example of verb-form development. The child begins to apply -ed to a few words appropriately, and then generalises this morphological marker to all past tense situations – for example: goed; ated. He then imitates some irregular verbs and begins to use these correctly. All adult efforts to teach 'went' and 'ate' are futile until the child himself has deduced these rules.

Therefore imitation is active and selective and involves comprehension. The child must recognise in the adult statement something which he knows and which is relevant to him. The only effective way to create production which is not merely parroting is to merge imitation and cognition (Crystal *et al*. 1976; Kretschmer and Kretschmer 1978; Ruder and Rice 1978).

Pointing out the child's error, and then providing an appropriate form:

Child: 'Me want...'
Adult: 'No, its not me want ... say 'I' want!'

It is interesting to note that adults rarely correct structural errors in children's speech during spontaneous communication, but rather concentrate on errors of fact. Remember that errors do not always indicate disability, as has been pointed out in the example cited under Imitation above. Natural errors may form part of the process which a child undergoes in order to deduce rules.

Dialects such as those used by minority groups abound in forms which differ from 'standard' English. Attempting to change or correct these structures may have a negative effect on a child who is just beginning to learn the value of communication (Crystal *et al*. 1976; De Maio 1983; Mellon and Caydan, cited by Kretschmer and Kretschmer 1978).

Finding the correct point between accepting 'errors' and indicating to the child that his communication is unintelligible or unacceptable is probably the greatest dilemma we face as remediators. However we must remember that people other than ourselves are going to converse with the child. It must be painful indeed for a child to discover that these 'others' do not comprehend or respond to his communicative attempts when his parents, therapists and teachers appear to do so. There is no magic solution to this dilemma. Perhaps one should be guided by the child's present communicative competence. Correcting his efforts when he is making his first tentative forays into the world of communication is destructive. The child's chronological age, the frequency of one's need to correct him, the milieu in which this is accomplished, and the degree of positive regard and trust between child and adult are all relevant factors in resolving this issue.

Vorce (1974) lists some 'corrective levels' for speech training which may apply to language teaching for the older child:

> The listener may indicate that he has not understood the message, and the child self-corrects.

> The listener may indicate a need for improvement: 'Say it again properly', and the child self-corrects.

> The listener cues the child to the specific correction required: 'I understand, but you forgot to say "is".'

> The listener pinpoints the error and then assists the child in correcting it.

The following four techniques are also useful for older children and adolescents:

Completion

Children are encouraged to complete items presented by the adult. For example,

> 'The girl wears a dress – the girls wear ....'

This may serve to teach grammatical rules or to increase vocabulary.

Replacement

The adult presents a sentence, and the child must replace an element or leave it out:

> Adult: 'The chair is big.'
> Child: 'The chair is old.'

(Kretschmer and Kretschmer 1978, p. 229.)

Alternative replacement

In this exercise a grammatical form must be replaced by a different form. For example, the child is asked to reproduce in the present tense a list of words taken from verbs in the past perfect tense.

Revision

Sentences are presented to be combined into new units. One way of doing this is to combine simple sentences using conjunctions.

For example, 'Choose the appropriate conjunction – and/ but/ if/ because – to join up these sentences:'

'His mother gave him a hiding. He stole the sweets.'

The forced alternative

This technique is described in detail by Crystal *et al*. (1976). The basis of the adult stimulus is formulated thus: 'Is it X or Y?' – the linguistic model is supplied, but the child needs to use both cognition and his already acquired linguistic skills to select the answer. If the forced alternative is at the appropriate level for the child, he will be able to respond.
Any grammatical form can be selected as the focus.

> **Target:** Verb
> Adult: 'Is the man sleeping or is he jumping?'
> Child: 'Jumping.'

> **Target:** Subject and Verb
> Adult: 'Is the man sleeping or is the boy jumping?'
> Child: 'The boy is jumping.'

This is an excellent technique, since it both complies with the rules of discourse and is flexible, but it also enables one to focus on the specific structure requiring remediation. However we have found it of limited value until the child has attained competence at Stage III on the LARSP. Perhaps the input is too complex before the child reaches this stage.

Verbal absurdity

We have found this to be a most useful method of eliciting language forms. Incorrect statements or ridiculous questions are used to encourage the child to recall lexical items or correct grammatical structures.

Point to a model pig and say:
'This is a cow.'

Indicate that you are joking and encourage the child to name the object correctly. Be careful not to do this until you are sure the child has learned the names of farm animals and can differentiate between them.

Show the child that his own output was communicatively inadequate.

Target:
SVO (Subject Verb Object):
Daddy is **kicking** the ball.

Child: 'Daddy ball.'
Adult: 'Daddy is **eating** the ball?'

(Miming the statement adds an extra dimension!)

Hannah *et al.* (1982) suggest asking questions such as,
> 'Do elephants fly?',
> 'Do aeroplanes bark?'

This auditory association task requires language processing skills.

Acting out the child's commands

This is another way to show the perspective of the listener.

Activity:
Instruct the listener to place objects in specific locations – put the ball under the table and the car on the shelf.

Child: 'Put the ball table.'

Adult: Indicate, by acting out the instruction and using the forced alternative, that the message is incomplete:
'On the table or under the table?'

Silence!

Why is it that speech–language remediators are unable to keep quiet?

So seldom do we allow children the opportunity to retrieve the structure they are trying to recall before we intrude. Grant the child the time to utilise his own strategies for language retrieval.

Silence, coupled with physical immobility, is also an effective tactic to encourage a conversational partner to act. Hold that mechanical toy out of reach, wind it up and sit immobile waiting for the child to command it to 'Go!' before you set it in motion.

Using one modality to cue another

Sign language (or the use of a manual code) is effective in assisting the recall of the verbal symbol through the use of another language modality.

Varying the context of the concepts to be learned

Teach each new concept within varied contexts.

> **Target:**
> The adjective 'soft'.
>
> **Activities:**
> Allow the child to see and feel a **soft** bunny, **soft** cotton wool and sit on a **soft** cushion. These must be contrasted in turn with **hard** objects.

Mastering a language is hard work for both pupil and teacher. However there is no reason why it should not be a game, an adventure, an interaction between two people allowing for the discovery of one another and of their own exciting hidden resources.

7. Equipment

As the medium of instruction in our programme is play, a range of appropriate toys, models and pictures must be available for assessment and therapy. However, in the present economic climate these items are exorbitantly expensive. We are aware that our readers may be working in a variety of contexts where the purchase of equipment may be impossible. You need to be reassured that you can improvise and create from waste materials to provide objects to which children can relate. Working with groups of children obviates the need for model dolls as subjects, and real household objects and school materials are far more effective than toys and models.

There are some excellent books which offer suggestions on how to use waste materials (old egg boxes, cardboard cartons and paper) to make model animals and familiar household objects. We refer you to:

1. Alison Spector and Helen Bengis, *Create From Waste!* Books 1 and 2.
2. *The Learning with Mother Series* (Ladybird Books).

For those readers who have an allotted budget with which to purchase equipment, here are some suggestions on how to select basic and relevant toys and books.

Everything you make or buy must be:

| **VERSATILE** | **DURABLE** | **APPROPRIATE** |

Versatile:
The item must be useful in a variety of linguistic contexts and activities.

Durable:
Unbreakable, washable. Cover all illustrations with adhesive plastic, or place in plastic sandwich bags.

Appropriate:
In terms of interest, age, sex and the cultural background of the child.

Here is a list of the most basic requirements for language therapy. If you are equipping a clinic or school you will need to consult a nursery school specialist to purchase appropriate construction toys, outdoor equipment and imaginative games.

Model dolls

These serve as the subject of clauses and phrases. Doll families with unbreakable bending limbs are commercially available. 'Barbie' dolls are not suitable.

You can easily and cheaply make your own family: use pipe-cleaners for trunk and limbs. Fix a bead on the pipe-cleaners for a head; paint features on the face and stick wool or hair on the head. Cut clothing from felt material (a back and a front), and stick these over the trunk and limbs. Dress father (a large figure), and son (a smaller figure), appropriately in pants and shirt. Mother and daughter must each wear a dress.

If you are unable to make or purchase family characters, use magazine pictures or cut-out dolls covered with adhesive plastic.

Body parts and clothing

There are a variety of commercially available products depicting the human body and clothing. These include flannel-graph kits made of paper or felt. An excellent set of plastic clothing and body parts to assemble forms part of the Peabody Kit (1977).

Make your own kit out of cardboard. Be sure to cut up the body parts – arms, legs, trunk, head – so that the child reassembles it as he learns to name each part.

Model animals

Realistic plastic sets of domestic and wild animals are available commercially. Make sure that these are relatively large. It is a good idea to purchase a double set of animals as you will need at least two of each species.

Again, you can, of course, use plastic-covered cut-out pictures.

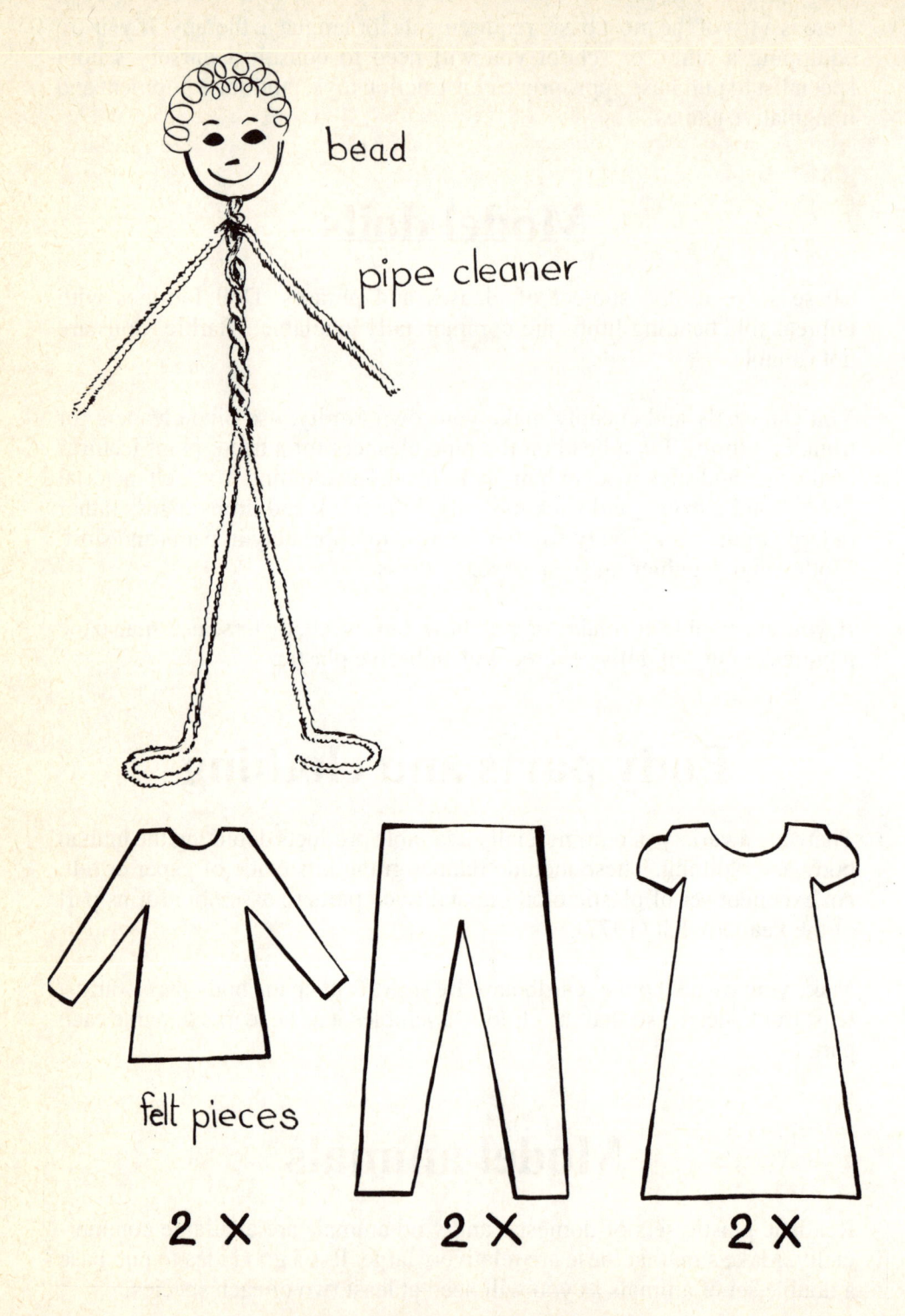

Figure 2: Pipe cleaner 'family'.

Other props

Model furniture, plastic fruit and vegetables; a variety of model vehicles (car, bus, plane, boat, helicopter, fire-engine, ambulance, police car, jeep, truck). Be sure that all the objects are culturally relevant if you are working with a young child. He needs to be familiar with the items in his own environment.

Mechanical toys

(To encourage vocalisation.)

Wind-up cars, battery-operated models, a Jack-in-the-box or any object that can be activated to move when the child vocalises. Model vehicles running down a sloping surface will suffice.

Tokens

Unifix cubes (Philip Lacey Ltd, N42-25); coloured discs; marbles; buttons; felt cut-outs; charms.

Miscellaneous

Balls, blocks, plastic monsters or insects. Magnetic toys can be made to perform all manner of interesting tricks on command.

Containers

A pillowcase; a child's suitcase; a basket; a variety of coloured boxes; a small 'house' made out of an old shoe-box. Be careful not to use plastic supermarket packets with deaf children, as they make a disturbing background noise.

A floor map

This is a most versatile piece of equipment. Add to it any of the local features with which the child is familiar.

Figure 3: Floor maps.

Commercially produced programmes

Two commercially produced programmes which we find useful are:

> *Three, Four, Five, Activity Books*
> MacDonald Educational, 1978.
> These booklets consist of clear, simple cut-out pictures depicting size, shape, colour and number concepts.
>
> *Wilson's Expanded Syntax*
> Educators' Publishing Service.

Books and pictures

Use a concertina file and file your loose pictures alphabetically (this does not apply to a phonetic inventory, of course). Here are some ideas for collecting relevant pictures:

The 'Talk-About' Series
Ladybird Books.

This series includes: Talk about holidays; animals; the park; the beach; babies; home; the garden; and others. The books are beautifully designed to include large, realistic pictures of the subjects, as well as sequence stories, colour matching, number activities and visual matching exercises. Purchase two of each book. By doing this, you can use every illustration. Cut up the books using the even-numbered pages from the first book, and odd-numbered pages from the second.

Back every picture with cardboard or newspaper so that the child is not distracted. Place all the large pictures in a plastic bag and file under A (animals), P (park) and so on.

Place all the number exercises from all the books in one pocket and do the same with the colours and shapes. Put all four pictures (cut separately) from a single-sequence story into a plastic sandwich bag. You will have a lovely collection of stories.

Illustration of verbs

It is always difficult to collect a realistic variety of pictures of actions. We refer you to an excellent little book with clear and amusing drawings, well arranged according to subject matter:

>Jack Kent, *Hop, Skip and Jump Book*
>Collins, 1974.

Story books

(You need to consult a librarian for a more extensive list.)

>Richard Scarry, *Best Word Book Ever* and *Storybook Dictionary, Great Big School House* and *What Do People Do All Day?* (Paul Hamlyn).
>These have very 'busy' illustrations, not suitable for easily distracted children, and not culturally relevant to Africa. They are delightful, however, and abound with lexical items of interest to children.
>
>Eric Hill, The *Spot* Series (William Heinemann).
>These books are fun for the young child as they have movable illustrations of doors that open, boxes that close, and so on. They are excellent for teaching prepositions.
>
>Louis Lensky, *Papa Small* (Oxford University Press).
>Clear simple drawings of household activities involving the whole family.
>
>*Beginner Books* (Jonathan Cape, Random House).
>These books are always well illustrated with delightful action-packed stories. They include the Bears Series, Barbar, and many others.
>
>*Captain Pugwash* is a favourite with the older or more linguistically advanced child. Publishers of this series are The Bodley Head.

In this book at the end of Book One, you will find a number of drawings that are designed for use by the therapist.

8. Home Visiting

Parents should be regarded as partners in the business of rehabilitating their children

In the United States and England there is now a network of therapists who are working with the communicatively-disordered in the family context. The orientation of their work has grown from a frustration with the minimal gains achieved by working within a one-to-one clinical framework.

We need to assume that parents want the 'best' for their children and that they know what 'best' is. As the family is ultimately responsible for their child, it is appropriate to encourage parents to adopt this responsible role in order to feel competent (Lund 1987).

'Language always occurs in a context and ... contexts are not all the same' (Gallagher 1983, p.1). Our programme has attempted to provide a variety of intentional contexts and linguistic contexts, but these occur within the confines of clinic or schoolroom. Real-life social contexts are the milieu in which children must use their language. The primary social context for the young child is the family, where language-learning normally takes place. The child communicates most frequently with family members.

Rustin (1987) says that if we do not study the family system when treating young stutterers, we are in no position to prescribe therapy at all. The programme must be tailored, not only for the child, but in accord with the family life style and system as a whole. Direct parent involvement in communication therapy provides a long-term management of the problem, and increases the probability of a carry-over of learned behaviours into varied social contexts (Mallard 1987).

Much has been written about the family system (Boscolo 1985; Minuchin 1974; Haley 1973), about the pragmatics of language (Lund *et al.* 1983; Gallagher 1983), and about conducting language therapy in the home. However there appears to be a paucity of literature on methods of evaluating the family system and its modes of communication in terms of the needs of a specific family member. Two excellent texts we recommend are *Deafness In The Family* (Luterman 1987) and *Working With Parents* (McConkey 1985).

It is clear that language therapy, conducted within a clinical or school setting, is of little value without family co-operation and participation.

Several attempts are made to ensure family co-operation and participation. Parents are invited to observe clinic sessions; home programmes are provided; parents are asked to observe and record certain behaviours in the home; and home demonstration programmes are sometimes offered in the clinic setting. In countries where services are government sponsored, therapists may visit the home on a regular basis. However in South Africa, which has limited manpower and financial resources, the latter is not always possible.

It is the writers' contention that a single home visit is worth months of therapy in a clinic, and should be a compulsory part of any rehabilitation programme.

Purposes of the home visit

Language environment

The term language environment applies to the social context in which the child communicates, and to the opportunities provided by this milieu for experiencing and observing new events leading to further language development.

The therapist needs to evaluate both facets with the family, and to assist them in creating situations conducive to language growth.

Family dynamics

Much has been written regarding the effect of a communicatively handicapped child on the family system and on specific members (Seligman 1983; Luterman 1987).

The birth of a handicapped child constitutes a crisis and families will vary in their solution to such a disruption in their lives. To assist families regain their homeostasis, it is necessary to observe family interaction 'with understanding and respect for the incredible complexity of human communication' (Webster 1977, p.2). Interacting with the family in their home environment provides *the family's* perspective of the child and his behaviours. On-the-spot solutions to problematic situations can be negotiated with the family, often with effective and lasting results.

Arranging for the visit

In the initial contract which you make with clients it must be understood that a home visit is part of the service. A frank explanation of its purpose and value must be supplied. Reassurance is offered that the visit does not in any way constitute an 'inspection', but is part of your attempt to get to know the family and to observe the child within the family context.

A specific time must be arranged for your visit, and care must be taken to obtain particulars such as the address and directions. Set limits in terms of the time which you will be spending with the family, and in terms of what they can expect you to do during your visit. One mother invited one of the writers for lunch as her home was at a considerable distance from the clinic. On arrival the therapist found that elaborate preparations for the meal were in progress – it was finally served at 3 p.m. She had been manipulated into prolonging her visit until the husband could return from work.

Of course it is preferable to have all the family members present, and this is usually possible when the visit is pre-arranged. Do not visit after hours or over weekends. You are performing a professional service and your clients must respect the fact that you have a personal life of your own.

How to conduct yourself

Encounters with families are a delightful experience of mutual exploration and self-growth. Approach your visit with interest and respect. You already have a shared experience and perception, for you too have a family of origin and can relate to the feelings generated by the client-family.

Show genuine interest and admiration for possessions or decor displayed in pride by family members – cultural artefacts may be of particular significance. It is useful at first to concentrate your interest on the children – this is less threatening for the adult members.

The children will inevitably want to show you their rooms and toys (ask permission of the parents before you accompany them).

This is always great fun, and provides a wealth of information for language activities.

Be sure to accept the hospitality offered to you. It is most offensive, particularly in the Indian culture, to refuse refreshment in the home. The way tea is served and the care taken over this gives you an insight into the light in which the family regards you. Often, over a cup of tea, revelations are made that are not easily forthcoming in a cold, formal clinic setting. Sometimes this is regarded as an occasion for mutual sharing: the family may ask you personal questions regarding your own household. These should answered freely; sharing the common burdens of child rearing, the cost of living, and other matters of general concern make counselling the human interactive process that it is. Nevertheless it is not helpful for you to reveal your interpersonal relationships in depth, especially those concerning your own family.

Leave-taking should be carried out with regard to the usual conventions – it is an affectionate exchange of thanks. Before leaving it is often helpful to summarise with the family things of importance which you have learned about them and their home. Of particular interest are objects that will be used to further the child's language development, and the new techniques which you have rehearsed with them for communicating with the child.

What to look for on the visit

The physical setting

The writers acknowledge their debt to Dr Donald Bloch MD, from whose teaching some of this information was gleaned. Dr Bloch conducted a workshop on family therapy in 1974 at Tara Hospital, Johannesburg. He is the Director of the Ackerman Institute for Family Therapy, and a past editor of *Family Process* (1970 –1982).

The neighbourhood

Families often travel great distances to reach the clinic. Petrol and bus fares are exorbitantly expensive, and the irritation of travelling with a tired and restless child is immeasurable. It is a humbling experience to undertake the journey taken week after week, and it affords the clinician a rare insight into one of the extra stresses caused by having a handicapped child.

The neighbourhood in which the family lives will offer some clues to the family's socio-economic status. If the family lives in a block of flats, it is helpful to note whether there are outdoor playing facilities for the children, or whether there is a park nearby. Your visit may well be an occasion for the neighbours to pop in. The support and companionship offered by friends and their children is often surprising to the clinician, who may have imagined the family to be isolated.

The home

The way people use and decorate 'their space' often gives much insight into how they feel about themselves, and how the family members view one another. Dr Bloch described a family in which the members had isolated themselves from one another. Although they lived in a two-roomed apartment, they had erected barriers of clothing-rails and furniture to compartmentalise their living space. In another home which he visited, the bedrooms were decorated in sombre shades of grey and black. We visited a home where every square inch of wall space was decorated with plaques and pictures, and rugs were two and three deep on the floors. There were enough expensive puzzles and toys to open a private nursery school, but these were meticulously packed in cartons, out of reach of the lonely little girl who was our patient.

Children may have their own bedrooms or share with a sibling. It is important that they have somewhere, however confined, in which to store their own special and private possessions. We made elaborate and secretive arrangements with one four-year-old sibling to store his treasured truck under the kitchen sink. We trust his two-year-old brother never did find out where it was hidden!

Children should feel comfortable to romp about in their home, but must learn to respect some areas as being the domain of their parents. Every home will reveal the values and interests of its inhabitants – we have seen a well-stocked and decorated bar-counter taking pride of place in one home, while religious artefacts adorned the walls of another dwelling. Bookshelves always reveal a wealth of information regarding their owners. For some, books are as much part of the daily activities as are the contents of the refrigerator, while for others books are rarely read but proudly displayed and cared for. Dr Bloch had the novel idea of asking the children to show off the medicine cupboard – he felt this supplied a wealth of information.

Homes have special features which may prove either advantageous or detrimental to a handicapped child. One mother had complained that her hard-of-hearing youngster refused to wear her hearing aids at home. The reason for this became painfully obvious when visiting the family at home. The floors were covered in attractive Italian mosaic tiles, and two rowdy siblings spent the afternoon riding their tricycles from one end of the house to another. No wonder Sarah could not tolerate the noise!

Gardens

Gardens are especially important features. There should be ample room for free play, without fear of damaging the flower beds. Sandpits are very easy to construct, and most families appreciate advice on how to maintain these. Swimming pools and fish ponds should be well fenced off – in one home we visited, the Wendy house was inside the swimming pool enclosure.

Toys: storage, care and use

With the mother's permission, enjoy being shown the toy selection by each family member. A broad selection of toys, no matter what the quantity, might often include the following:

Unbreakable toy cars, trucks, balls and bats, soft cuddly toys and dolls

Children enjoy displaying these about their rooms, or having them stored in a large rummage-box or basket. It is fun to tip these out regularly, sharing them with friends and siblings. They are easy to pack away at the end of the day.

Tricycles, wagons and bikes

Families generally have rules regarding the possession of these toys – where they are to be stored, and where they may be ridden.

Cutting, pasting and drawing materials

These must be large enough for young children to manipulate. Blackboards are useful and encourage children not to draw on walls and furniture. It is very easy to paint a blackboard on a playroom wall.

Constructive toys – blocks, Montini, Stickle-bricks, puzzles

These are the most difficult to care for at home. They should be stored separately in plastic containers. Plastic storage bottles are commercially available, but are rather expensive. In some homes these items are not well cared for and pieces of puzzles appear amongst the rummage toys. This is a great pity, as children learn so much by completing a puzzle or construction. Children also learn a great deal about caring for their possessions and those of others if they assist in packing away the toys in the correct containers at the end of the day. Easy-to-reach shelves offer the best storage for these items, and nursery school teachers are helpful at giving advice in this regard.

Books

These should be age-appropriate with brightly coloured, clear illustrations for young children. These too should be well within reach and displayed on shelves. Children must learn to care for their books and look forward to daily story reading with one or the other parent.

A special selection of books and toys may be stored out of sight and reach. It is always good to have something new to play with on a rainy day or during an illness.

Clinic-talk with the mother often revolves around how to stimulate the child, but this is the only sure way to explore the child's world and the mother's ability to organise it.

Clearly the range of toys available in the house depends upon the socio-economic status of the family. In lower-income families the above variety of toys will be too expensive to be afforded. The *Create from Waste* books mentioned above (Chapter 7, Equipment) may assist you in making suggestions for activities in these homes.

You need to join in with the children in discovering ways to utilise their own toys to develop their language. Often the mother has not realised what a wealth of material she has at home. She needs to be reassured that there is no need to purchase new and expensive equipment – show her how to utilise what the family already has. We discovered that an eleven-year-old deaf client had a passion for 'Star Wars' characters, and invited him to bring his model collection to the clinic. Language therapy was designed round the outer-space theme, and the child became a willing participant.

The home visit is also an excellent opportunity to encourage siblings to play constructively with the handicapped child. Older siblings, in particular, are delighted to be included in a stimulating programme.

Pets

Part of your visit will also surely revolve around the family menagerie. Much has been written, with good reason, about using animals as language facilitators in rehabilitating children. It is a good idea to call the mother's attention to the rich lexicon that may be derived from this source:

> Names of animals; the noises they make; characteristics (beaks, claws, fur, tails); textures and colours (soft, sharp, grey, brown); where they live (cage, kennel, basket); what they eat, and so forth.

We have known children to run through their speech repertoire with the family dog when co-operation with therapist and family members has not been forthcoming. Rapport is easily established at the clinic when you can name and enquire after the pets you have met at the child's home.

Family interaction

As has already been stated, home visiting is a unique opportunity for observing the interaction between family members. We are constantly amazed at the misconceptions about relationships which may be conjured up in a clinic setting. Families often cope far better with a handicapped child than expected, and joining them at home to solve behaviour problems is far more effective than trying to imagine what the situation is really like for them. If grandparents play a major role in the family, they should be invited to be present during your visit.

We often give advice concerning child-rearing practices without any idea of a particular family system and its beliefs, or of the specific ethnic and cultural factors that may determine how children are expected to behave. Taking tea with the family at home will give some insight into these individual or group styles.

A critical issue is family communication, particularly pertaining to your own client. Questions you should ask yourself are:

> What is the level of communication expected of the child by each family member?
>
> How does he have his needs met?

Is he using the level and type of communication you expect from him at the clinic?

Observe the listening skills of family members. Do they give the child sufficient time to communicate? Do they indicate by non-verbal means (body language) that they are impatient or irritated when he demands their attention?

Is the handicapped child in fact demanding too much attention? If not, how much more can you demand of him and the family, given the particular family dynamics and the many demands placed on it at home?

Examples

– Mrs Smith felt guilty that she was not constantly responding to Simon's oral attempts, but her two younger children (one a six-month-old) required her attention. She and the therapist needed to plan a time when Simon could have her undivided attention.

– John's father, Mr Jones, was speaking to him in lengthy seven-word utterances when he had only just mastered single words. After we had worked with them both in the garden, Mr Jones soon learned to bring his utterances down to a realistic level.

– Mrs Roberts complained that she was the only family member demanding speech from Greg. This was understandable, considering that nobody else in the family had observed his therapy sessions. When Greg demonstrated his capabilities at home for his father and his brothers, they were spurred on to make far more demands on him.

Demonstrating how to make full use of an everyday activity (frying an egg, for example) gives an opportunity to work with both mother and child on communication strategies to teach language.

Record-keeping

Write a full report on each visit, covering all the aspects discussed in this chapter. It will assist you to clarify your thinking about the family, the child and his communication.

Share your report with the family on subsequent visits. You will then reach consensus regarding the matters that require attention. You will be able to identify family mobilisation points and to formulate initial goals. Select procedures that are congruent with the family style, and allow the parents to be part of the decision-making process concerning therapy (Andrews and Andrews 1987).

9. School Visits

As the child may spend more than half his day at school, it is important for you to maintain a close association with his teachers.

With the parents' permission, make an appointment to visit the school during the morning so that you can observe the child's interaction with teachers and peers. The teacher is a professional colleague and should be treated as such. However, there are bonds of confidentiality between you and your clients, so that there may be aspects of the case which you are not free to discuss.

Ask permission to observe the child in class before you hold a discussion with the staff. In this way you will observe his communicative and social interaction. As during the home visit, you will want to know how the child communicates, with whom, and how effective his receptive and expressive communicative competence is, especially in a noisy, busy environment. The hard-of-hearing child is particularly at risk. He resorts to much subterfuge to keep up with the class, and teachers will often assure you he can hear well, when in actual fact he relies heavily on cues other than her oral commands. Teachers rarely stand still in a specific position in the classroom, so even lip-reading is precarious.

It is helpful to test this out with the assistance of the teacher. Ask her to issue specific commands to the children as she is moving about, and test the child's ability to respond to these on his own. At one school we visited, the teacher had the novel idea of asking each child the name of his dog. The hearing-impaired child was incapable of repeating any of the names without contextual clues.

In the nursery school environment it is imperative that you observe a structured 'ring'. Ask the teacher to tell the children a story, or to discuss a subject of interest with the group. She must then question the children on the contents of the story or discussion. She can encourage commentary and discussion among the children. You will be able to gauge whether the child you are observing hears and/or comprehends the communicative interchange. We often find that the hearing-impaired child may follow the teacher's discourse with difficulty, but that he does not hear the other children at all. (It is essential that an F.M. system be used in formal nursery groups as well as in the schoolroom.)

This sort of exercise is helpful in giving the teacher insight into the child's limitations. After she has given you her impressions of the child's social behaviour and scholastic attainment, you may offer her your assessment of his communicative abilities. Communication, socialisation and learning are intimately bound together – the rehabilitation of a single one of these aspects cannot be effected without due regard to the others. Pool your resources to assist the child. Be sure to maintain contact with the teacher throughout the therapy process. You may want to use school subjects to facilitate language, and your language therapy should facilitate scholastic achievement.

Summary

In Book 1 we have looked at some important underlying principles of effective language therapy. By far the most important one is that of **assessment**. Detailed accurate initial assessment is worth its weight in gold, and not only provides the fundamental information about what to proceed with, but where and how to proceed.

We have also examined the **components of a therapy session; the importance of planning and reception;** relevance and context, and creating motivation. Specific **language techniques** are discussed and illustrated, and reference is made to suitable **equipment**. The importance of **home and school environments** is also considered.

Language rehabilitation has to take place in the broader context of the child's environment with other significant people playing a substantial role. The therapist may be viewed as the facilitator, ensuring that the natural context of the child is optimally attuned to his needs and the process of rehabilitation. How to achieve this will be described in Books 2 and 3.

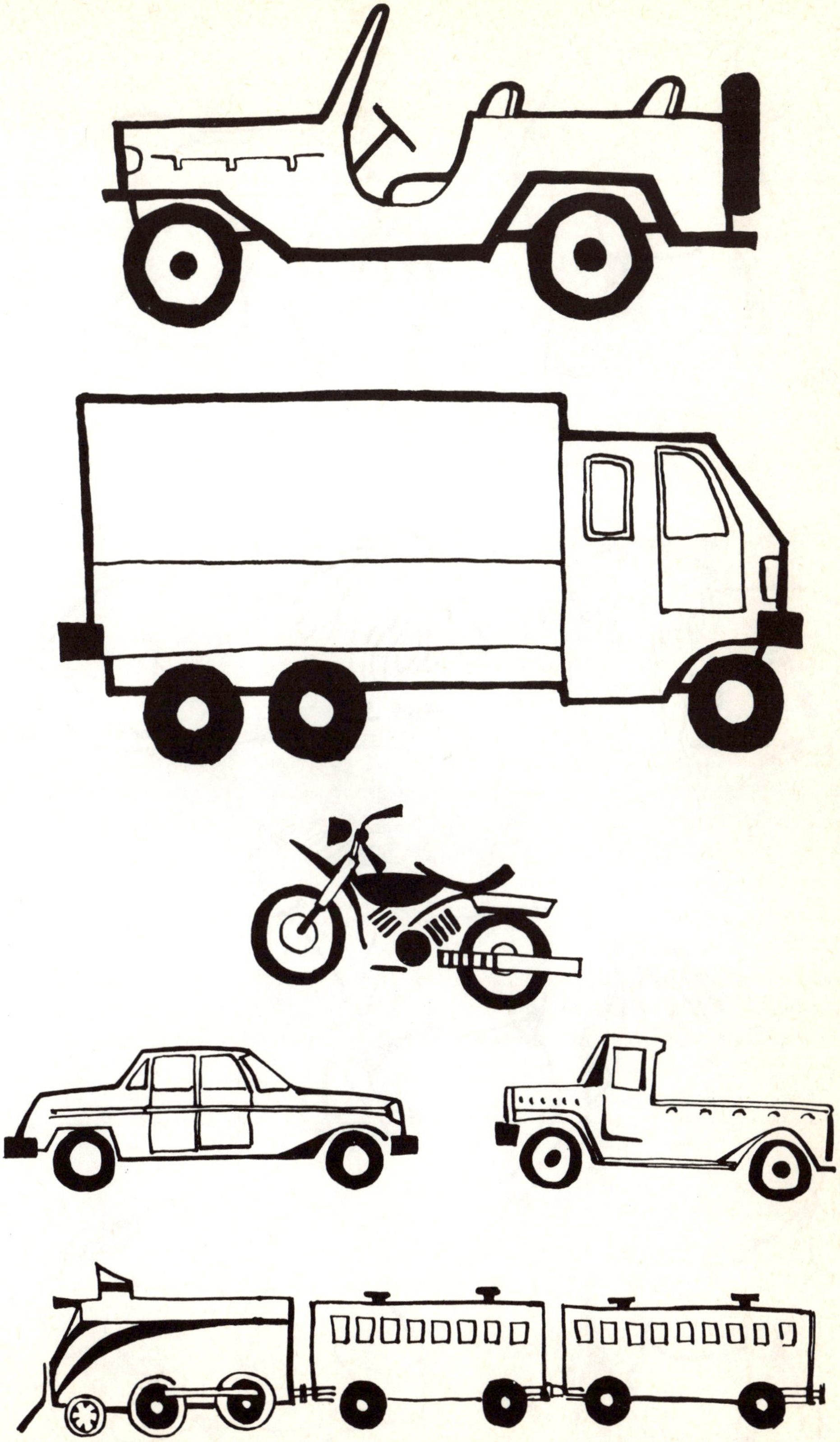

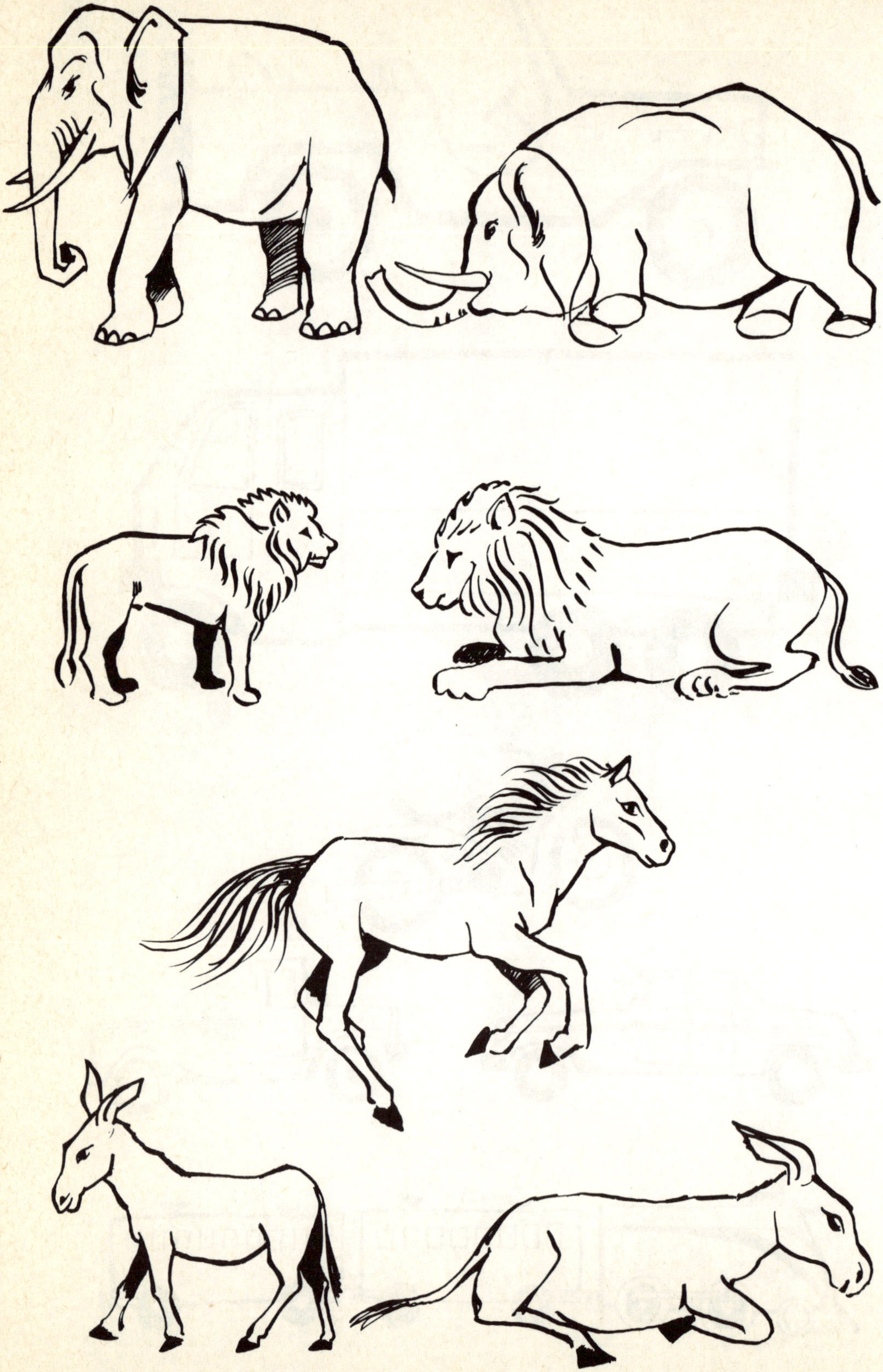

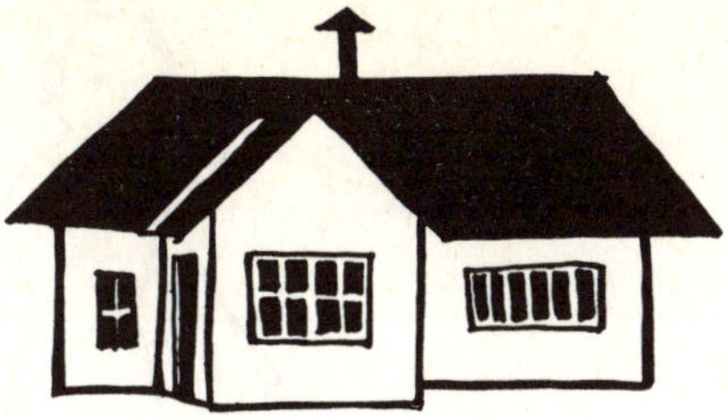
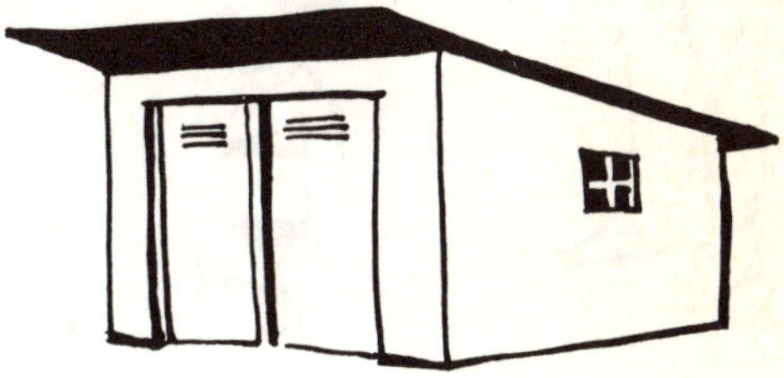
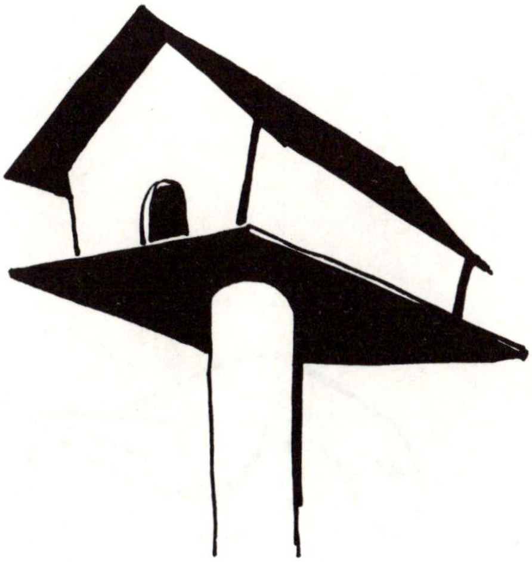
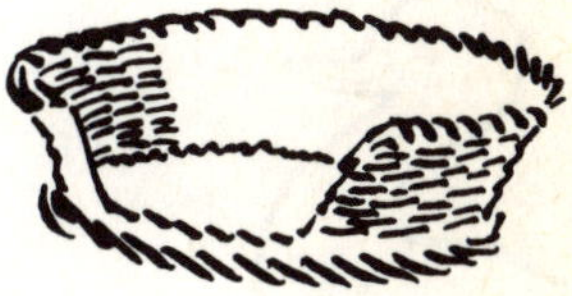
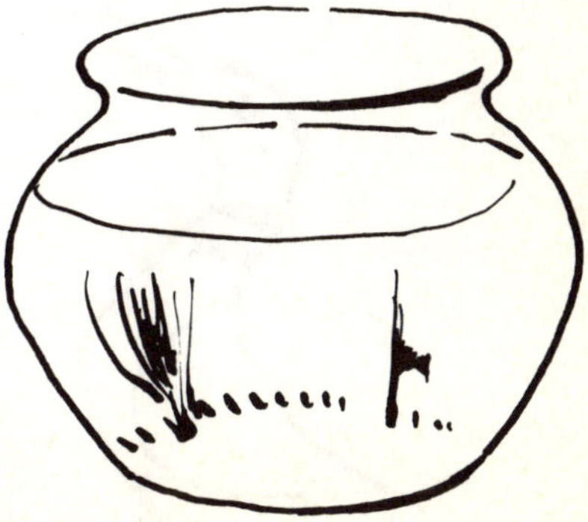
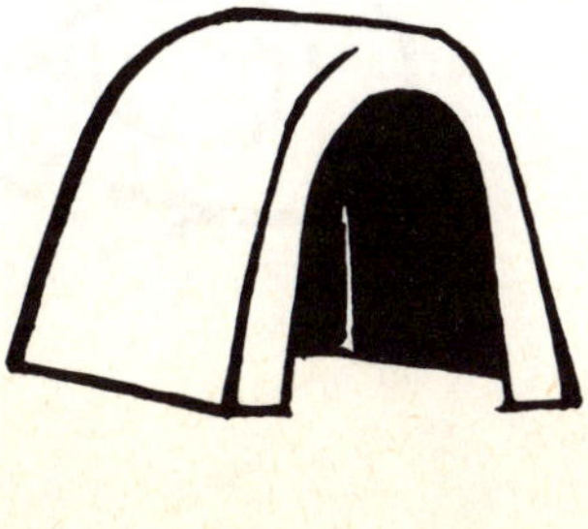

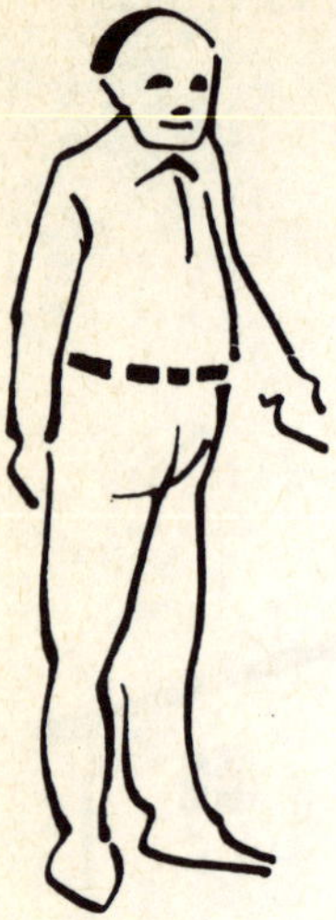

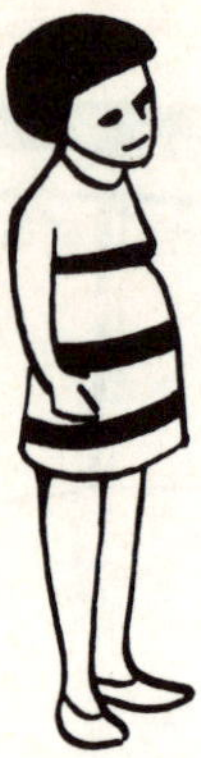

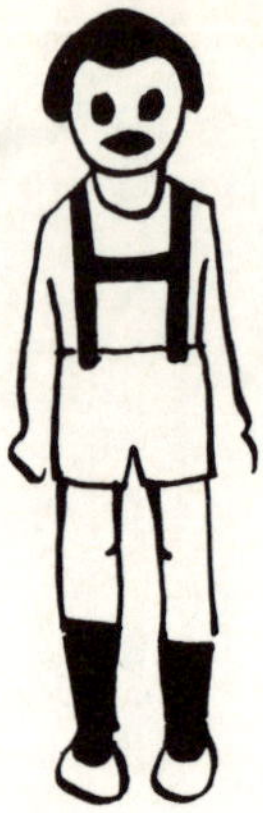

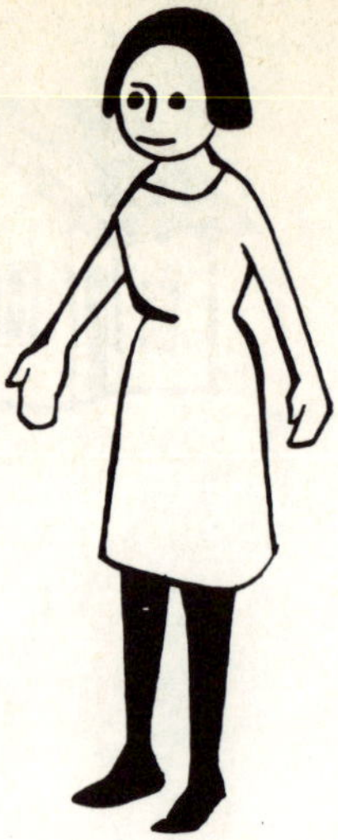

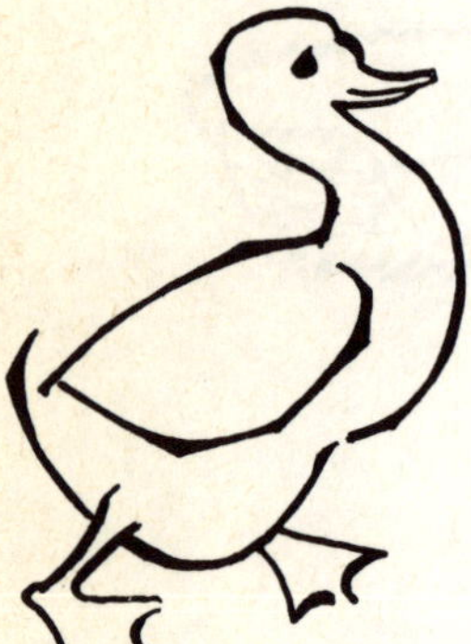

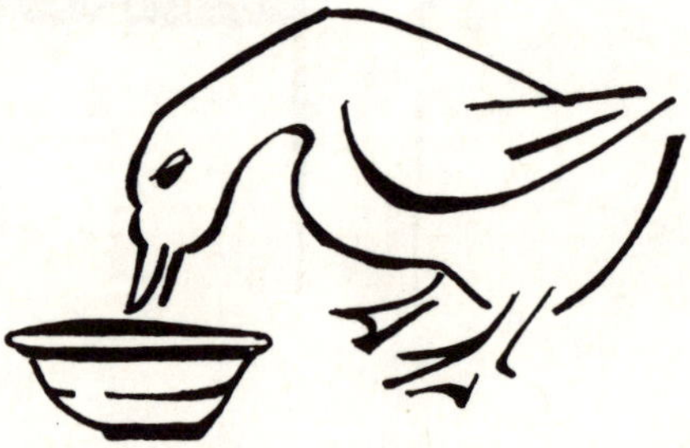

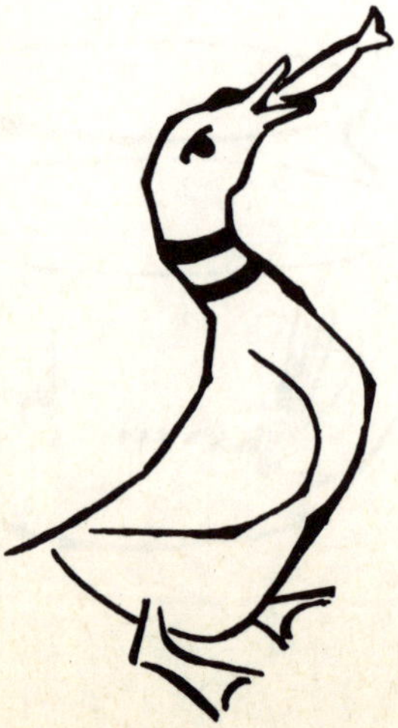

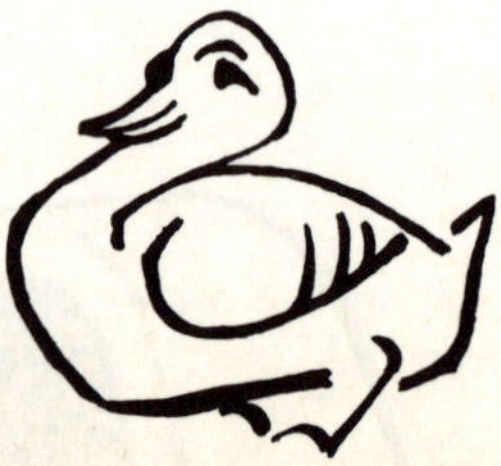

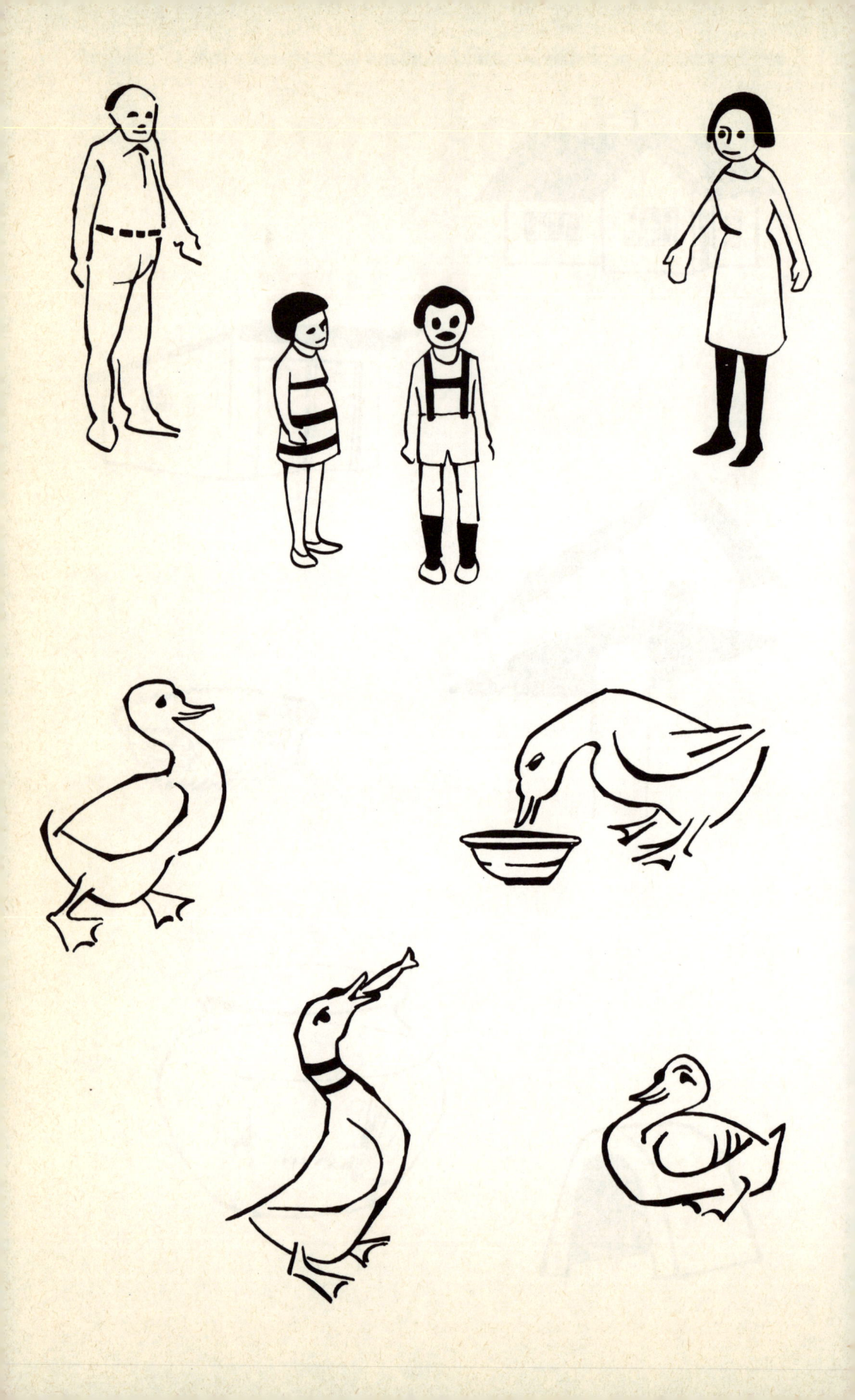

BOOK TWO

LARSP - TECHNIQUES AND SUGGESTIONS FOR EACH STAGE

1. Vocalisation and the First Lexicon

Introduction

Having provided the seven-stage framework for LARSP in Chapter One, we will now consider each of these stages in turn, providing practical suggestions of how to remediate each stage.

Where to begin therapy and what equipment to use will obviously depend on the child. Again, these suggestions are intended as guidelines, and should not be viewed as a substitute for original and individually-planned therapy.

The first stage in acquiring words is a two-way process in which children's vocalisations are responded to by care-givers, who in turn stimulate language development.

Most of the writers in the area of pre-linguistic development, among them, for example, Bates (1976) and Prutting (1982), suggest that the most important precursor to language development is the development of intentionality; that is the way the child seems to convey intention through communication. This the child learns to do throughout his first year by vocal, gestural and verbal means. As early as six months of age, normal children are able to recognise the names of familiar persons and things, and by the age of about nine months to a year children may use their first word or sign.

Intervention should occur at the pre-linguistic stage in order to assist the primary care-giver in maintaining dialogue with a seemingly non-responsive child. Deaf children in particular may be unaware that oral stimuli are significant, and parents may need to learn manual symbols in order to communicate.

Many texts advocate talking to young children in 'full sentences', as words supposedly acquire meaning in context, and the child must learn to decode a 'whole sentence' (Simmons-Martin 1976; Courtman-Davies 1979).

The counter-arguments to this advice abound:

> 1) It is necessary to modify one's input to the child's level of linguistic competence.
>
> 2) In the case of the language-impaired child unable to process lengthy utterances, word boundaries must be as indefinable as a Chinese sentence is incomprehensible to an English-speaker.
>
> 3) For the hearing-impaired child who receives an incomplete auditory signal, 'The cat sat on the mat' will sound like 'ə æ æ on ə æ ' How is the child to fathom where words begin and end? Perhaps the black furry object is an 'æ', but then the flat floor covering must surely be a 'æ' – incomprehensible and too vague to store and recall.

Huttenlocker (1971, p. 321) states: 'The confusion of the small child as to exactly what a single word might be expected to be, is greatest with sequences made up of words that have not been used in isolation.'

If, when the child learns language, the linguistic stimulus which he receives is just one step ahead of his own expressive competence, it stands to reason that the input for a non-verbal child should be a **single-word utterance**.

However, having used a word in isolation with varying prosodic features to denote the intentional context:

> 'Ball?' ('Where's the ball?')
>
> 'Ball!' ('That's a ball!')
>
> 'Ball' ('Give me the ball!')

– the utterance may well be expanded in order to elucidate context:

> 'Up, ball!'
>
> 'Where's the ball?'
>
> 'The ball's gone!'

(See Book 1, Chapter 6.)

Encouraging vocalisation

The first step on the road to communication is responding to the infant's communicative attempts, allowing him to set the topic by vocalising, signing or simply gesturing and pointing.

If the goal is to teach him an oral symbolic system, then specific activities designed to highlight and differentiate his oral productions are recommended.

Engage in babbling interchange

Much has been written on the significance of babbling in the first year of life, and care-givers are always encouraged to spend a lot of time and energy babbling and cooing to their infants.

However, when an older child babbles or resorts to jargon in an obvious effort to communicate, we, as therapists, respond to him with meaningful dialogue and attempt to shape his utterances into words. We have had some experience with children who for various reasons do not use coherent oral communication, and we have found it expedient to begin by communicating on the child's level, rather than insisting that he changes his communicative mode at once. Two such children in our clinic – one hearing-impaired and one emotionally disturbed – spent at least six sessions babbling companionably with the therapist. After this period, during which no intelligible speech was used by either child or therapist, parallel play activities were introduced. Seated with her back to the child and provided with her own pile of blocks, the therapist vocalised 'up, up' as she constructed her own block tower. Each of the children began chorusing her output. This period of parallel play was followed by joint efforts to construct a bridge out of blocks, where the children appeared to tolerate meaningful verbal interchange at last, until finally the therapist was able to demand a single-word output from them in order to regulate their environment. The model presented by De Maio (1983) describes this programme in some detail.

Onomatopoeic words

These are useful in encouraging vocalisation, as they are easily repeatable by the young child, and are clearly significant in the child's early language and experiential environment.

Materials:
Select onomatopoeic words, or models to represent them: Wow-wow (dog); meouw (cat); moo (cow); um-um-um (plane); quack-quack (duck); hop-hop (frog/rabbit).

Activity:
Sit beside the child. (In the case of a hearing-impaired child this discourages lip-reading and encourages listening skills.) Produce one toy at a time, activating it appropriately while vocalising its name. Then encourage the child to activate the toy, vocalising appropriately as he does so (Crawford 1979).

Voice-activated toys

Materials:
a) Any toys that are mobile, for example a Jack-in-the-box or mechanical toys.
b) Constructive nursery toys such as rings on sticks, peg-boards, buttons to post in a bottle.
c) A model car to run down a sloping tray or a table-top.

Activity:
Hold the toy out of the child's reach. Issue a single-word command to the toy or object:
'Jump' (jack-in-the-box); 'go'(car); 'off' (before taking a ring off a stick).
Immediately, activate the toy accordingly. Any command is appropriate, provided that you use the same command whenever you play with a particular toy.
Allow the child to activate the toy, hoping that he too will issue the command. If he does not do so, reverse roles. Vocalise for him as he presses a lever or pops a button in the bottle, but when it is your turn hold the toy out of his reach and pause expectantly, waiting for him to issue the command.
At first any attempt to vocalise should be rewarded by action, but slowly shape the child's output by providing a model in your own speech, and expect him to use an intelligible utterance.

Use of a mask

In this activity the child learns to associate purposeful vocalisation with an attractive cardboard mask.

Materials:
Draw a happy face on a large, round piece of cardboard.

Activity:
Hold the mask several inches in front of your face so as to ensure that your voice is not muffled. Babble behind the mask and then offer it to the child to do likewise. (A further incentive is added by asking the child's mother to babble first.)

Use of vocalisation in pragmatic contexts

When the child is able to vocalise on demand, begin teaching him to do so within a social context. At this stage it is vital to enlist the co-operation of his entire family. Up to this point the non-verbal child has communicated by means other than oral symbols. He now has to learn the effectiveness of an oral symbol system however rudimentary it may be. Reward only his oral demands. The accuracy of word approximation varies within the bounds of individual development from child to child.

The child wants an apple which is out of reach on the table. Previously he would gesture, pointing and using jargon to indicate his need. Respond to him by showing you know what he wants, but do not give him the apple. Model the word for him several times: 'apple!', playing the role of listener and speaker. Use the technique of silence and immobility to show him that it is his turn to 'explain' his needs. When he approximates the word 'apple', give it to him.

In a busy household, with the intervention of other family relationships, this becomes a very stressful stage in the therapeutic process. The family will require a lot of support. As a therapist you will need to negotiate with the family concerning the amount and frequency of such demands on the child.

2. LARSP – Stage I

Crystal (1982) divides Stage I into minor and major sentences.

Minor sentences

These sentences are 'non-productive', implying that the elements are unable to combine with other elements according to grammatical rules. Minor sentences include:

Responses:
'Yes', 'no', 'ummm'.

Vocatives:
These are calling signals, like 'Mommy!'

Other:
Vocalisations performing social functions, like 'ta!', 'bye-bye!'

Stereotypes:
We include this category in Stage I rather than considering it as 'problematic' (Crystal 1982). Stereotyped sentences are utterances in which all or part of a construction has been learned as a single unit, like 'gimme' ('give me'), or rote-learned nursery rhymes.

Major sentences

There are three major communicative sentence types – statements, questions and commands. **N**, **V** and **other** refer to items that appear to be used as nouns, verbs or other grammatical forms. (The reference to 'problems' is omitted here, as our interest is not in analysis, but in remediation.) **Q** refers to wh-questions like **what**, **where**. **V** appears in the column 'commands', and refers to verbs as imperatives, such as 'jump!'

The first words

We need to supply the child with a core of lexical items upon which to build his syntax.

The selection of a lexicon

The foremost determining factors in selecting items are interest and relevance. Chronological and mental age are factors likely to affect interests, and the child's own personal needs, and his unique environment will dictate the relevance of objects and activities to him.

Always collaborate with the care-giver when selecting first words, as this individual is most familiar with the child and his environment. A very young child will not be able to generalise, so that the only 'wow-wow' he may identify will be the large pink furry toy on his window-sill. Conversely he may not have differentiated within a category, so that all four-legged animals will be called 'wow-wow'.

This highlights the need for you to familiarise yourself with the child's unique world (see Book 1, Home Visiting). We ask the mother to bring a selection of the child's own toys with her to therapy until the child is mature enough to identify unfamiliar objects.

Words need not be selected according to simplicity of production. A 'long' word such as 'elephant' may be your first choice if this is the child's favourite toy. However we are aware that phonological complexity can interfere with semantic development, and it is therefore preferable to select easy-to-say words at this stage.

Foodstuffs are not usually among babies' first words as they eat a minced variety of foods, vegetables and meats, better known as 'num-num'. Clothing is also of very little interest to the child. Objects may be conflated, so that 'bottle' is more easily identified as 'milk'. Select the term favoured by the mother, and encourage her to use this consistently.

Family names are notoriously idiosyncratic – we have had more pet names for grandmothers in our clinic than we care to recall.

Cultural factors will also play a part in word selection. Types of dwellings may well vary according to the culture or demography and your lexical selection must take this into account. There is ample opportunity to teach the older child about this variety as you develop your theme-teaching.

Use a 'baby-register' with the young child. Words such as 'moo-cow', 'doggie' and 'Mama' may well serve to 'lure the infant into language'(Ferguson 1977).

For the deaf child, a further consideration may be the visibility of words on the lips, or their relative audibility – words containing low-frequency sounds being the easiest to hear for most deaf children. Using a total communication approach tends to overcome this problem.

How to introduce early lexical items

Gillham (1979) offers three discrete levels which are to be combined as an indispensable part of the learning process for teaching new words:

1) Demonstrating:
focusing the child on the word and its referent.
2) Choosing:
getting the child to select the word from several others.
3) Using:
bringing the word into context.

Cognition precedes semantics, so that the child must understand a concept before he labels it.

Nouns

Allow the child to select the topic. As he points to or looks at an object – his bottle, his teddy – name it and give it to him to explore with all his senses.

For the deaf child, hold the object close to your face while you name it, and simultaneously sign. If the child is sufficiently mature, match the object to its picture as well as to other similar objects to encourage generalisation.

Repeatedly name the object, varying your intonation with your intention:

>'Ball?' ('Do you want the ball?')
>'Ball!' ('There's the ball.')

Then use simple utterances such as:

>'Here's the ball!'
>'Where's the ball?'
>'A big ball.'

Encourage the child to play appropriately with the object – throw the ball for instance.

At this stage words are selected according to the introductory comments made in this chapter, and not according to their relationship with one another. In order to pace the programme and ensure that the child is retaining the lexicon, test his retention by making him select an item which you name from a choice of two or three objects. Luria (1971) believes that until the age of sixteen months the child will be unable to make such a selection between conflicting stimuli, and will be attracted by the object rather than by the communicative stimulus. However, by changing both stimuli on each successive trial, we have been able to elicit correct responses from children as young as nine months of age, the child riveting his gaze on the named object.

For the older child, three to four items may be used. A 'postbox' into which he is required to place the correct object or picture is often a sufficient source of motivation. If the child does not select the named object correctly, do not allow him to place it in the box. Say to him:

'No, not the shoe – I want the ball.'

This counteracts frustration and serves as further reinforcement of the chosen stimulus. Always allow the child to play with the correctly selected object if he wishes to do so, otherwise the testing situation tends to become rigid and punitive. Occasionally, one needs to resort to a token or edible reward when the task is successfully completed (see Expanding the Lexicon, below, for further information).

Verbs

(See Book 3, Verbs.)

Always select action verbs at first: jump, fall, dance!

> Ask the mother to hold the small child on her lap so that he faces you. Give a single-word command, using an uninflected verb: 'Jump!'. The mother immediately responds by lifting the child into the air. Be certain she has waited for your command before acting. After several trials the child usually begins to respond without the mother's assistance.

Actions must always be carried out by the child himself. Family members should be enlisted, with puppets, dolls, stick-figure drawings and photographs – all useful props. However, Lassman (1950) offers a word of warning. She cautions that activities should always be varied and appropriate to their context: 'A child can become so weary of bowing and hopping day after day, in the same place and for no apparent reason, that the practice can lose its value!' Remember that children use only uninflected verbs at Stage I.

Other (major sentences)

The writers have found that prepositions and adverbs of place are the most relevant emerging grammatical forms for the young child to master. These forms lend themselves to repetitive actions, and should be practised in a variety of contexts. Be sure that the child can manipulate the equipment you select, or he will become too easily frustrated. Also ensure that he is capable of comprehending object permanence if you hide objects 'under' or 'in' a container. (For a detailed discussion of prepositions and adverbs, see Book 3.)

Questions

These must be demonstrated only in context at this stage. 'Who?', 'What?' and 'Where?' are the first developing wh-questions.
Children use single words with rising intonation to ask yes/no questions: for example, 'Car?' ('Are we going in the car?').
(For a detailed discussion of questions, see Book 3.)

Minor sentences

Respond to all vocalisations as if they were significant. Greetings such as 'hello' and 'good-bye' are encouraged by modelling, waving and so forth. Discourage embedding these utterances: for example, 'say "bye-bye" '. This tends to mask the target, the latter being more effective in isolation.

Respond promptly to 'ta' (meaning 'thank you' or 'give it to me'). Play-formulae using stereotyped utterances such as 'peek-a-boo' and 'clap handies' often lure children into dialogue.

Expanding the lexicon

This is an ongoing process, and is often mistakenly associated with pre-school language remediation only. Comprehensive lexicons appear in many texts, and we refer our readers to the following:

> 1) Mary Courtman-Davies, *Your Deaf Child's Speech & Language*. The Bodley Head, London, 1979.
> The author supplies an excellent list of diverse grammatical forms – nouns, verbs, prepositions, adjectives etc. This is a relevant lexicon for young children.
> 2) David Crystal, *Profiling Linguistic Disability*. Edward Arnold, London, 1982.
> In this book David Crystal presents his PRISM (Profile in Semantics) which is an attempt to provide semantic profile charts. One such chart, PRISM-G, deals with the relationship between semantics and grammar. The other, PRISM-L, relates semantics and the lexicon. We have found the latter chart to be a particularly useful guideline for lexical development in therapy.
> 3) Geoff Keays has recently published a local version of the first thousand words in English, Afrikaans and Zulu, which is highly recommended (Struik 1988).

Our own system of classifying the lexicon

This is according to subject matter, and may be loosely classified into Primary, Secondary and Tertiary vocabulary.

The primary lexicon

This includes all items of interest in the child's immediate environment: body parts; clothing; family members (Daddy, Mommy, the names of siblings and pets); animals - pets, domestic farm animals and wild animals; toys and vehicles. Also included are first action verbs (jump, sit, fall); first adjectives and adverbs (dirty, big, naughty, quickly); and early prepositions (in, on, under, up).

The secondary lexicon

By now the child has moved into Stages II, III and IV on the LARSP, and will show an interest in an environment further afield from his home and daily living – the road (postbox, pavement, traffic); shopping (trolley, money, chemist); the park; the zoo; the beach; the airport; the harbour; the station; people and their occupations (the fireman, the nurse); family relationships (brother, cousin, father); time and seasons (winter, tomorrow, a week); and religious days or festivals (birthday, New Year).

All projects must include descriptive terms and actions as well as nouns: monkey, elephant, rabbit – climb (up/down) feed, walk, big, soft, fat, lazy, sharp (horns); brown, grey. Where do they live? What do they eat?

The primary and secondary lexicon is a useful reference list upon which to build. Keep expanding each category as the child matures and develops. The two-year-old may only be able to name 'eyes, ears and nose', whereas the five-year-old may have sufficient competence to learn about 'elbows and eyebrows' and 'what's inside'(our hearts pump blood).

The tertiary lexicon

Often the speech pathologist is so preoccupied with assisting the young language-delayed child with a basic lexicon that she loses sight of the extensive vocabulary used by normal language learners. It is a sobering experience to spend the morning in a regular nursery school, listening to five-year-olds discuss 'Star Wars' and the 'A Team'!

Books, and television, are the magic gateway to these imaginative worlds, as well as to the real world beyond the child's immediate experience.

Although we are focusing on the acquisition of a spoken (or signed) lexicon, we must not lose sight of the close relationship between the spoken and the written word. According to Butler (1984), reading is dependent on the syntactic use of language structures, and narration is dependent upon semantic as well as episodic memory.

The child's own verbal-narrative skills are an excellent vehicle for testing his verbal comprehension as well as his semantic competence and memory. His future mastery of the printed word rests upon these abilities.

Story-telling should be a delightful two-way process, designed to increase and diversify the lexicon and to encourage the use of more complex grammatical forms.

Stories and books

The increment of the lexical repertoire

Having expended energy on such items as 'toothbrush', 'shoes' and 'bus', it is time to move on to the enchanting world of folklore and life in other lands. Every child should be familiar with 'Humpty Dumpty', 'Red Riding Hood', with giants, 'cops and robbers' and pirates. Select books from your local library and encourage parents to do so. Librarians are trained to assist in the appropriate selection of books for children. The primary factors which must influence your selection are age and interest, since even the most involved story can be reduced to a simple language level. When the plot is dependent on a play of words or a situation beyond the child's comprehension, change the theme to suit your need. The 'Little Red Hen' went to unbelievable lengths to acquire sufficient flour for her bread – the agricultural process may be beyond the child's comprehension, but the social interaction in this plot is obvious!

Use sequence cards to teach the well-loved nursery rhymes as some of their vocabulary is obscure:

> 'Little Miss Muffet
> Sat on her tuffet
> Eating her curds and whey...'

Four clear pictures depicting a girl sitting beneath a tree to eat her breakfast, the arrival of the spider and rapid departure of the young lady may be described thus:

> 'Look – there's a girl. Her name is Miss Muffet. What is she doing? Sitting and eating! What's that? A spider! It's big and ugly. She's afraid. She jumps up and runs away. All her porridge is spilt!'

As an introduction to the world beyond the child's experience, draw a **ground map** with pictures or models of his home, neighbourhood and city (see Book 1, Equipment). Teach him his address with this map, then extend his horizon by discussing his country and other lands. Read about children of other lands, their dress, their dwellings and their lifestyle. Books dealing with this theme abound, and children are fascinated by them. Before 'reading' the book, discuss new vocabulary to avoid interrupting the flow of the narrative.

Increasing comprehension and the use of grammatical forms

Ensure that the child attends, comprehends and participates. Seat the hearing-impaired child opposite you to ensure that communication is total. Conceal the book while introducing the topic. This way the child is not distracted by the illustrations. 'This is a story about a naughty boy.' Now, show him the illustrated cover to reinforce your statement.

Proceed through the sequence of events, being careful to reveal each illustration only after your verbal description. Allow the child to participate. Ask relevant questions and discuss the action in the narrative.

'That's the boy's sister. Do you have a sister?'

Try to use newly acquired grammatical forms in your story. If you have just taught regular past tense, select a story containing verbs such as walk/walked, cry/cried, hop/hopped, and stress the -ed verb form.

The child's own narration

Lahey (1988) views children's narrative ability as developmental, and stresses the importance of assessing and remediating this vital and frequently used communicative form. She defines narration as 'the production of increasingly larger sized connected units.' Narratives may be the description of everyday events, and they do not only involve formal story telling. In order to master narration, children require language knowledge, a capacity for concentration and 'world' knowledge. They also need to keep the listener's interest and perspective in view. Lahey stresses the fact that narrative skills are vital for social interaction and scholastic success. Language-impaired children often experience great difficulty with narratives. They 'recall less information, display errors in sequencing, are less explicit in giving information, have poor use of cohesive devices, and demonstrate more communication breakdowns.' (Lahey 1988). Adults tend to judge children's stories as successful if there is a logical sequence of events. Lahey describes several other facets which are equally important. She enumerates all of these facets along a 'narrative chain' in which content and form interact. She believes that there is no normative data or narrative development, but only trends. Lahey also cautions that different cultural backgrounds will elicit varying narrative styles concomitant with the varied expectations of the listener.

There are various ways to elicit stories from children. Butler and Sawyer (1985) describe several of these:

> 1) The easiest way to elicit a story is by using **sequence cards** (see Book 1, Equipment). You may arrange these in order yourself; tell the child the story which the cards depict, and ask him to repeat it. Other formats include:
>
>> a) Placing the cards in random order before the child, asking him to rearrange them in correct order, and then to tell the story.
>> b) Omitting the final card and asking the child to describe how he thinks the story may end.
>> c) Suggesting several endings and allowing him to select the final card best depicting your description.
>
> 2) Tell the child a story without pictures and ask him to 'tell it back'. Lahey (1988) cautions that this is not a natural way to tell a story.
>
> 3) Ask for an account of 'what happened in school today', or 'what you did on your holiday'. This form of narration usually fosters episodic rather than semantic memory, but it is a first step to story-telling.
>
> 4) **'Story maker'**
> Use a picture to introduce a subject: 'John's bike is old. He wants a new bike. What will he do?'
> Encourage the child to complete the story imaginatively.

Lahey (1988) suggests further ways to elicit stories:

> 1) Complete a story stem: The child is given the stem of a story and asked to complete it:
> Once upon a time there was a king...'
>
> 2) Spontaneously generated stories may be captured by placing a tape recorder at the family dinner table.
>
> 3) The examiner and child may co-construct a story.
>
> 4) Peterson and McCabe, cited by Lahey, have seventeen pre-prepared topics which they present to the child whilst he plays:
> Tell me about your dog...

We need to work on the components of narration: attention spans; world knowledge; and language knowledge (content, form and use). Children should not only be exposed to frequently presented and appropriate stories, but the manner of presentation itself is vital. The language stage used by the interlocutor should not be too complex for the child (see Book 1, The Importance of Reception).

Acting out stories may be helpful. Using the structural format of well known stories such as *The Three Little Pigs* or *The House that Jack Built* may also help children to construct their own stories.

Metalinguistics, reading and writing

According to Butler (1985), the development of metalinguistic skills in young children is a prerequisite for reading and writing. The child needs to step back from the meaning of language and be able to look at its form. In order to foster this skill, Constable and Van Kleeck (1985) offer some basic suggestions to therapists and teachers working with the young child. These may be applied as follows:

> 1) Give the child the notion that print is meaningful. Do this by reading the simple print, moving your finger below it as you do so whilst the child sits next to you and follows the story.
> (This is a contradiction of the method described for fostering verbal comprehension in the preceding section on story-telling. As each technique is designed to develop different skills they should be used interchangeably.)
>
> 2) Model the functions of print. Point out to the child that instructions to characters in the story may be illustrated in written form: 'That says "Stop!".'
>
> 3) Introduce basic conventions of print: for example how to hold a book; reading from left to right, and from beginning to end.
>
> 4) Introduce basic meta-lingo-words such as: **talk**, **listen**, **say**, **tell**, **story**, **word**, **letter**. Model and encourage very early metalinguistic skills in the context of narration. Children must become aware that words are a separate

entity from objects. Make up nonsense words; point out that some words sound funny, for example, 'glug-glug'; or that words may be long while the object which they represent is not – a train is a long object, but the word is a short one.

5) Encourage children to 'write' their own stories, even if they have a limited ability to do so. As a preliminary to this, print the child's verbal description of his own drawings for him, using his own words (Ewald 1985).

3. Stages II – IV – Developing language complexity

Some clinical considerations

Remember to work horizontally across the LARSP, simultaneously introducing clauses, phrases and morphological markers into varied sentence types (questions, statements and commands).

When stimulating the child, supply a syntactically correct model one level above the child's level of competence. The child will continue to produce ungrammatical utterances as he deduces rules and expands his linguistic abilities.

The writers have described structures recorded on the LARSP that are syntactically incorrect, recognising that they accurately reflect child language development. However, these structures are not targets for teaching English, and should not be taught as such.

The activities described in this chapter are designed for use in a structured clinical or school milieu. Model dolls and contrived situations must substitute for real life. Children need to communicate in a variety of communicative contexts. Clinical work is valueless if 'carry-over' into these social contexts is not achieved. This can best be accomplished by working with parents and others with whom the child interacts.

Each structure will be presented as follows:

1) Definition of the structure in terms of grammatical form

2) Examples of the structure

3) Activities – including the materials to be used. (Several variations are suggested for each element of the struc–ture so as to encourage the child to 'generate'.)

> **SVA** Daddy/Mommy/ the boy is going/riding/driving to the shop/work/home.
>
> 1) Varying the subject:
> Daddy/Mommy/the boy is going to the shop.
>
> 2) Varying the verb:
> Daddy is going/riding/driving to the shop.
>
> 3) Varying the adverbial:
> Daddy is driving to the shop/home/to work.

The adult is expected to give a correct model, but it is anticipated that the child will omit certain elements. These elements appear in the text within brackets. No attempt should be made to teach these elements until the appropriate stage of development has been reached.

For example:
(The) boy walk(s) to school. That('s) his dog.

Note the use of the contracted forms in the adult model: **that's, I'm, it's**. This is in accordance with normal conversational style. The use of total communication will assist the hearing-impaired child master these forms which he may not hear.

Teachers working with groups of children in classrooms have expressed concern that our programme may only be effective in a one-to-one clinic situation. This is definitely not so. We have enjoyed playing our games with classes of hearing-impaired and language-impaired children. It is only essential to use the model doll family subjects when working with a single child. It is far more effective using the group of children themselves as the subjects. They learn one another's names, and thoroughly enjoy playing 'teacher' to the rest of the class.

4. Stage II

Clauses

Commands

VX: The verb plus any other part of speech:

Jump up!
Fall down!
Hug Mommy!

Activity:

Target:
VS: Jump/sit/fall Mommy/Daddy/frog!

Materials:
Model family or animals.

Activity:
Command the models to act. First vary only the subject:
'Jump Mommy/Daddy/frog!' and to activate the models appropriately.
Then vary only the verb:
'Jump/sit/fall Mommy!'
Finally vary both elements:
'Jump/sit/fall Mommy/Daddy/frog!'
Be sure to allow the child an opportunity to issue each command.

Target:
Vpart: Jump/climb up/down; come in.

(See V part, Stage II.)

Questions

QX: Wh-question plus any other clause element:
What('s) that?
Where('s) Daddy?
(For activities see Book 3, Questions.)
Remember to vary one element at a time at first:
'Where('s the) car/man/ball?'
'What('s)/who('s) in (the box)?'

Statements

SV: Subject Verb:
Daddy/Mommy jump/fall.

This implies that Daddy jumps or is jumping; Mommy falls or is falling.

It is preferable to omit the present continuous **is** and **-ing** in your model as it clutters the utterance. On no account must the child be expected to use is and -ing or third-person agreement at this stage.

Activity:

Target:
Mommy/Daddy/Joe eat(s)/sleep(s)/sit(s).

Materials:
Model family or animals; model furniture and food.
Place the models at one end of a table and activate each one in turn, ensuring that you keep the verb constant.
Label the action:
'Daddy/ Mommy sleep(s).'
After the child has demonstrated that he can activate each subject to 'act', either on his instigation or yours, introduce another verb or two and encourage him to use the target utterance appropriately. (It is helpful to use verbs requiring props at this stage, such as a chair, a bed etc. as children are often unable to improvise.)

SO: Subject Object:
Man car.
This girl a sweet.

These ungrammatical utterances are typical of developing child language and can only be understood in the context in which they are uttered. 'Man car' may mean,

'That man has a car'
'The man gets into the car'
'The man pushes the car'

depending on the event which the child is commenting upon. If the child produces this utterance when attempting a more advanced structure, it must be considered developmentally sound. However, avoid producing such ungrammatical utterances in therapy. It is preferable to emphasise the target words in a short but grammatically accurate sentence.

SC: Subject Complement:
That('s) hot.
Me Johnny (I'm Johnny).

Activity 1:

Target:
Me Gary/I'm Robyn/you('re) Peta.
Although pronouns do not appear at Stage I, you may introduce the first person singular pronoun here as a stereotyped social response, along with naming. Point to each other or to other group members and name:
'I('m) Robyn, you('re) Peta.'
Accepting incorrect pronoun cases, let the child name everyone present:
'Me Peta – you Robyn.'

Activity 2:

Target:
This (is)/that('s) big/small.
(See Book 3, Determiners.)

Neg X: Negative plus any other clause element:
Not Daddy, no train, not run.
(See also Book 3, Negatives.)

Activity 1:

Target:
Non-existence of an object:
No apple. (In context: there is no apple – it has disappeared!)

Materials:
An apple, a box or a cloth.
With the child's assistance, hide the apple in the box or under the cloth, saying 'apple – go under!' Without the child noticing, remove the apple. Open the box – lift the cloth – and express surprise at the apple's disappearance. Model the target and encourage the child to imitate:
'No apple.'
Leave the apple in its place in some of the trials to enable the child to contrast presence/absence, existence/non-existence.

Activity 2:

Target:
Desire:
No apples. I don't want the apple. I don't want a banana.

Materials:
Any two objects – a banana and apple, a model car and plane. Offer the child a choice between two objects, presenting the less attractive one first. Assist him in his refusal:
'No apple – banana!' ('I don't want the apple – I want the banana').

Activity 3:

Target:
Denial:
No car; not (a) car – a bus.

Materials:
A small selection of objects which the child can name.
Hold up one object at a time, and misname it:
'(Here's a) car!' (holding the ball).
Enjoy the joke along with the child and assist him to say:
'No (t) (a) car – (a) bus.

AX: Adverbial plus any other clause element:
Shoes there, put on (your jersey).

Activity 1:

Target:
Pig/cow here/there.

Materials:
Model farm animals, several locations (a barn, a house, a box).
Walk each animal into a barn or house commenting:
'Cow – there; pig – here.'
In order to keep the noun constant at first you may use several animals of one species:
'Pig here, pig there.'
Using the target utterance, let the child place all the animals.

Activity 2:

Target:
Shoes/pants on/off.

Materials:
The child's own clothing or a doll to dress and undress.
Model the target while dressing and undressing the child or doll, then allow the child to do likewise, verbalising as he does so.

VO: Verb Object:
Want (a) sweet, push (the) car, cut (the) apple.

Activity 1:

Target:
Want (a) sweet/ice-cream.
This is probably the most frequently used statement in a child's repertoire, and should be exploited to the full! Encourage family members to withhold response to demands until the child not only names the desired object, but uses this clause:
'Want (a)...'
The polite form: 'Please, I want a ...' is redundant and confusing at this stage, but is easily taught at a more advanced stage of language development.

Activity 2:

Target:
Pull/drive/push/(the)bus/car/lorry.
Cut/eat(the) apple/banana/bread.

Materials:
Model vehicles; a selection of foods; a blunt knife.
Instruct the child to 'cut the apple/banana/bread', or 'push the bus/car/lorry', making sure that he selects the object you have named. Reverse roles – the child must instruct you to act. When he has mastered this, place all the objects together before him, and vary the verb. This ensures that he has responded to both the verb and the object.
This activity may be carried out using any transitive verb (one which takes an object). The following are examples of the transitive verb: wash, eat, cut, peel, bite, kick, throw, catch, roll, sweep, wipe, clean, fix, break.

VC: Verb Complement:
Be hot, meaning: It's hot, I'm hot.

As the child has not yet acquired the auxiliary at this stage, it is not really valid to teach him 'is hot' ('it's hot'). However, as with the structure SC, you may feel entitled to introduce this as a stereotype. Use the following activity:

Target:
Is big, is small, is broken, is pretty.

Materials:
Pictures depicting the attributes of a big flower, a small flower, a broken flower, a pretty flower.
Turn the pictures face down, and allow the child to describe each one as he turns them over:
'Is big, is small.'
Use the question intonation before he does so:
'Is big? No – is small.'

Phrases

DN: Determiner noun:
My ball, that man.
(See Book 3, Determiners.)

Adj N: Adjective Noun:
Big ball, red car.
(See Book 3, Adjectives.)

Activity:

Target:
Red/blue/yellow ball/boat/plane
or
Big/small ball/boat/plane
or
Dirty/clean ball/boat/plane.

Materials:
A red boat, a red ball and a red plane; a yellow boat, a yellow ball and a yellow plane; a blue boat, a blue ball and a blue plane. Any objects will do, providing there are three of them, each a different colour.

Make sure that the child knows the colours and can name the objects. Place all three boats in a container and ask the child to give you one as you name it. Reverse roles so that he may use the target utterance:

'(A) red boat.'

Then place all the boats, balls and planes in the container so that the child is compelled to respond to both the adjective and the noun. Vary the activity by using picture cards depicting the objects. Place the cards face downwards and guess which is which before turning the picture over:

'(A) red boat?'
'(A) yellow plane?'

Repeat the activity using big and small objects, or dirty and clean ones.

NN: Noun plus Noun:
Mommy('s) bag, Daddy('s) shoe.

This is a precursor to the later-developing genitive (see Word, below). At this stage include the necessary inflection(s) in your model, but don't expect the child to use them.

Target:
Baby('s) bottle, Daddy('s) car, (the) boy's ball, Mommy('s) hat.

Materials:
Model doll family and varied objects appropriate to the characters, for example a bottle for the baby. Place all the models and objects before the child. Select an appropriate object and give it to a doll, modelling:
'Mommy's bag.'
Allow the child to share out the objects using the target utterance. You may have to keep the subject constant at first, giving all the objects to a single character:
'Mommy's bag, Mommy's brush.'
Alternatively, vary the subject and use a single object:
'Mommy's sweet, Daddy's sweet.'
Variation:
Select objects which are not character-specific: banana, apple, orange. The child must then choose to whom he will give each fruit. Remember, the child must not be expected to use the possessive s at this stage. He is likely to say:
'Mommy bag.'

Pr N: Preposition Noun:
In (the) box, on (the) table.
(See Book 3, Prepositions.)

Be sure to vary only one element at a time and introduce the prepositions in varying contexts.

VV: Verb plus Verb:
Make (something) run, want (to) see (something).

This is ungrammatical, but view it in context, and accept it as developmentally sound if produced by the child whilst attempting a more complex utterance.

Verb plus particle:
Look up (my friend), sit down.

Target:
Look up, sit down, fall down, come in, go out.
(Be careful not to confuse these with the verb + the prepositional phrase, such as: Look up the chimney.)

Materials:
A puppet, a doll's house or a container.

Activity:
Command the puppet to 'sit down', 'fall down', 'come in', 'go out'.

Int X: Use of an intensive form with any other element:
Down there, very sore, too many.

Activity 1:

Target:
Very dirty/clean.

Materials:
A washable doll.
Plaster the doll with mud, helped by the child, commenting:
'(It's) very dirty! Very clean!'

Activity 2:

Materials:
Marbles, smarties, buttons.
Pour a quantity of the selected objects into a container:
'(It's) full!'
Keep on pouring until it's overflowing:
'Too full!'

5. Stage III

Expansions

Clause elements may be expanded by phrases.

> **X + S: NP**
> A two-element clause has its subject expanded by a noun phrase:
> Big man run, black shoe dirty.

Combine any of the noun phrase activities listed for Stage II with another single element. The phrase must be in the subject position.

Activity:

Target:
The big/small pig/duck eat(s)/walk(s).

Materials:
A large and small model pig, a large and small model duck, a model trough.
Activate the pigs to walk:
'Big pig walk! Small pig walk!'
Command the pigs, but let the child activate them appropriately. Reverse roles so that the child uses the target utterance. Introduce another variable:
'Big pig/small pig walk/eat.'
Finally vary the noun:
'Big/small pig/duck eat/drink.'

> **X + V: VP**
> A two-element clause with expansion of the verb phrase:
> Boy is sleeping, me want to go.
> (See activities listed for SV and VO at Stage II, and Book 3, the Verb Phrase.)

X + C: NP
A two-element clause has its complement expanded by a noun phrase, clause or adjectival construction:
Is a car, it very old.

Activity:
See **SC** Stage II. Repeat the activity, but expand the Complement.

Activity:
Describe each object:
'That(s) a long/short string/worm.'
Allow the child to do so too, then hide the objects in a box and have fun feeling each object without looking at it. The object must be described before the 'player' may pull it out of the box:
'Is (a) long string, is (a) short worm.'

X + O: NP
A two-element clause has its Object expanded by a Noun Phrase:
Kick the ball, cut this banana.

It is more natural for the young child to expand the objectival rather than the subjectival phrase, and this structure should therefore be introduced before **X + S: NP**.

Activities:

Combine any activity to teach a noun phrase, listed for Stage II, with any other single element. The noun phrase must be in the objectival position.

Activity:
Target:
Throw/roll/bounce/kick this/that ball.

Materials:
Several balls, either with identical features, or if further expansion is targeted, then with differing features: a red ball, a rugby ball, a cricket ball.
Place all the balls in a container and instruct the child to:
'Kick/throw the big ball/that ball/the tennis ball.'
Introduce variables according to the child's level of competence.
Reverse roles so that the child gives the commands.

X + A: AP
A two-element clause with its Adverbial expanded by an Adverbial Phrase:
Walk down there.
Sit on the chair.

Activity 1:

Target:
Walk down there/climb up here.

Materials:
A puppet, constructions made of blocks.
Instruct the puppet while activating it:
'Walk down here, climb up there.'
Allow the child to issue the instructions.

Activity 2:

Target:
Sit/stand on/under the chair/table.

Materials:
A puppet, two or three items of furniture.
Instruct the puppet or the child himself to act. Reverse roles and allow the child to give the instructions:
'Sit under the table, sit under the chair.'
Be sure to vary only one element at a time:
'Sit under the table/chair.'
'Sit/lie under the chair.'
'Sit on/under the chair.'
When the child is able to both decode and encode the instruction, vary all the elements at once:
'Sit/lie/stand under/on the table/chair.'

Clauses

Commands

VXY: Verb plus any two other elements:
Draw (a) nice house now.
Put (the) cup here.
Any activity listed for **VCA**, **VOA** and **VO$_d$O$_i$** may apply to **VXY** when the target is presented as a command.

Let XY: 'Let' plus any two other elements:
Let the pig/cow in/out.
Let Mommy/Daddy in/out.

Materials:
A doll's house, a fenced enclosure, model dolls and animals.
i) Shutting the dolls in or out of the house, instruct the child:
'Let Daddy/Mommy in/out.'
ii) Enclosing the animals within the model fence, assist the child to instruct you:
'Let the pig/cow in/out.'

Do XY: 'Do' plus any two other elements:
Do/don't touch that!

The positive form, 'Do stop that!', 'Do go home', is not used in South African English, but the following are frequently in use:
'Do some more', 'Do (up) my shoe', 'Do the puzzle', 'Do it again'.

Activity 1:

Target:
Do it again.

Materials:
Any mechanical toy.
Allow the child to activate and reactivate the toy, repeatedly commanding him to 'do it again'. Then take the toy and activate it yourself, pausing between turns so as to encourage the child to tell you to 'do it again'.

Activity 2:

Target:
Do (up) the button/zip/bow.

Materials:
Commercially-produced felt books with buttons, zips and bows to manipulate.
These are easily made out of scraps of material. You may use a doll with the necessary clothing. Take turns in instructing one another to 'do (up) the bow/buttons' etc.

Questions

QXY: A Question Word with two other elements of clause structure:
What('s) Mommy doing?
Who('s) in the house?
(See Book 3, Questions.)

Activity 1:

Target:
What('s) (the) boy doing?

Materials:
Activity picture cards – a boy jumping, a boy hopping, a boy running.
Place the cards face downwards and play a guessing game. Each selecting a card, the 'player' asks:
'What('s) (the) boy doing?'
Answer:
'Jumping!'
Note that the child should be using the verb form 'jumping' at this stage.

Activity 2:

Target:
Who's in the box/house?

Materials:
Model dolls, a box and a doll's house.
Using only the box at first, the child hides one doll in it. Ask:
'Who's in the box?'
Guess:
'Mommy?'
Encourage him to reply:
'Yes/no.'
Reverse the roles so that he gets to ask the question, and to guess the answer. Then introduce the doll's house together with the box, ensuring the appropriate use of the full question:
'Who('s) in (the) (doll's) house?'
'Who('s) in (the) box?'

Variation:

Ask:
'Who's in the box?'
Encourage the child to open the box and say:
'Mommy!'

VS(X): A question is formed by inverting the order of the Subject and the first part of the Verb Phrase. If there is a third element of clause structure it is labelled **X**:
Is he kicking (the) ball?
(See Book 3, the Verb Phrase.)

Statements

SVC: Subject plus Verb plus Complement:
(The) man is cross.
(That) man is (a) policeman.

Activity 1:

Target:
(The) girl is dirty.
(The) man is cross.
(The) balls are big, etc.
(See also SC in Stage II.)

Materials:
Picture cards depicting attributes of objects and people. Make sure that each subject is depicted with several attributes; for example have a picture of a cross man, another of an old man, yet another of a happy man. Another set of cards should depict two or more subjects displaying the same attributes, to be used for the plural auxilliary **are** – two girls who are dirty, two girls who are happy etc.

Describe the pictures using the full target utterance. Test the child's receptive and expressive competence by allowing him to select a card you name, or to describe the cards himself. Let him place the appropriate card in a post-box for motivation. Place two cards depicting opposite attributes face down. Allow the child to select one card and to conceal it from you. You may ask:
'Is (that) man big?'
Target response:
'No! The man is small.'
Reverse roles if he is able to cope with the question form.
(See Book 3, Questions.)

Activity 2:

Target:
That/this man is (a) policeman/fireman.

Materials:
Pictures of people and their occupations.
Having taught this new lexicon by explaining and describing the occupations, make certain that the child can identify each 'actor': a policeman, a nurse, a doctor. Turn the cards face downwards and guess who is in the picture before revealing them:
'(This) man is (a) policeman.'
The one holding the greatest number of correctly guessed cards at the end of the game is the winner.

SVO: Subject plus Verb plus Object:
Mommy push(es) the pram.
I love you.

Activity:

Target:
(The) boy/girl ride(s)/pat(s)/feed(s) (the) horse/ donkey/elephant.

Materials:
Model doll family and model animals.
Place a single 'subject' (a boy) and several 'objects' (a horse, a donkey, an elephant) before the child. Take turns in commanding the subject to act:
'Boy, ride the donkey/horse/elephant.'
Be sure not to vary the verb as yet. When the child has mastered this target, vary the subject as well as the object:
'(The) boy/girl rides (the) donkey/horse/elephant.'
Finally vary the verb:
'(The) boy/girl rides/feeds (the) donkey/ horse/elephant.'
(See **VO** in Stage II for a list of transitive verbs useful for teaching this structure.)

SVA: Subject plus Verb plus Adverbial:
Mommy come now.
Daddy drives fast.

Activity 1:

Target:
Daddy/Mommy drive(s)/run(s) fast/slow(ly).
The horse/rabbit run(s)/walk(s) fast/slow(ly).

Materials:
Model doll family, model animals, a model car.
Select a single subject, Daddy, and activate the doll to drive the car fast and slowly:
'Daddy drive(s) fast – Daddy drive(s) slowly.'
Then vary the subject – Daddy/Mommy. Whilst you describe the activity, let the child select and activate the correct subject.
Reverse roles so that the child uses the target utterance.

Variation:

Target:
You run/hop/walk there/here.
You jump/climb in/out/under.

Materials:
Any object into which the child can climb.
Instruct one another according to the target utterance:
'You climb under'.
'You hop there.'

Activity 2:

Target:
(The) lion/elephant/giraffe stand(s)/lies/walk(s) behind/under.

Materials:
Model animals, a bridge constructed out of blocks.
Using a single subject, the elephant, place it behind or under the bridge:
The elephant stands under.
You cannot use the phrase 'under the bridge' at this stage as the expansion of an adverbial phrase with two other elements does not manifest itself until Stage IV. Vary subject, verb and adverbial, until the child can respond correctly to your utterance and use the target correctly himself.

Neg XY: The Negative plus two other elements:
Not ball go.
No gone sweet (meaning 'I still have the sweet').

Like Neg X in the previous stage, negation still falls outside the sentence. It is not until Stage IV that the child is able to negativise a specific element within the sentence (eg. Neg V or Neg X). You may want to substitute correct grammatical structures if the child's language has developed sufficiently:
'The sweet('s) not gone.'
(See Book 3, the Negative.)

VCA: Verb plus Complement plus Adverbial:
Is dirty now (meaning, 'it's dirty now').
Is gone again (meaning, 'it's gone again').

Activity 1:

Target:
Is/are dirty/clean now/later.

Materials:
Two washable dolls, model animals or furniture.
Enjoy smearing the objects with mud as you model the target and encourage the child to imitate you:
'(It's) dirty now/ (it) (will) be clean later.'
(Note that the use of the pronoun **it** is introduced so as to produce a syntactically correct utterance.)

Activity 2:

Target:
Is gone again.

Materials:
A Jack-in-the-Box or puppet.
Activate the toys to disappear into a box or behind a screen while you model the target and encourage the child to imitate you:
'(It) is gone again!'

VOA: Verb plus Object plus Adverbial:
Put (the) book there.
Take (the) cup away.

Activity:

Target:
Put/hide (the) book/pen/ball in/under/behind (the box).
Using a single object at first, instruct one another to:
'Put/hide the pen in.'
(As in the structure SVA you cannot use the adverbial phrase 'in the box' as this constitutes an expansion with two other elements. The child will not be ready to cope with this yet.)
Vary the object and adverbial when the child has mastered the first target:
'Put/hide (the) pen/book/ball in/under/behind.'
This activity is fun when there are more than two 'players'. The first and second players instruct one another to hide the objects, while the third player waits outside the room. He must then find the hidden objects by asking:
'Where's (the) book?'

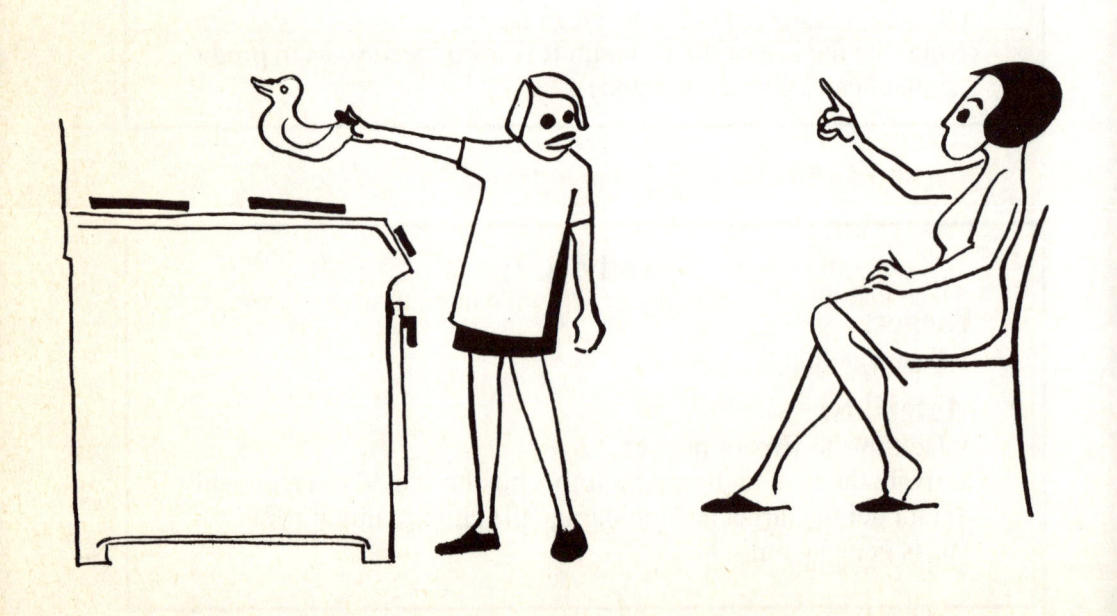

VO^{d}O^i: Verb plus Direct Object plus Indirect Object:
Give (the) ball to Daddy.

Activity 1:

Target:
Give the ball/bucket/ring/bottle to Daddy/Mommy/Baby/(the) girl/(the) boy.

Materials:
A variety of objects such as those listed in the target; a model doll family.
Group the family and the objects in two separate corners of the table. This assists the child to classify the direct and indirect objects of the clause. Instruct him to:
'Give the ball to Mommy.'
'Give the bucket to Daddy.'
You may have to keep one variable constant at first. If so, use a number of the same objects – several balls, several sweets:
'Give (a) sweet to Mommy.'
'Give (a) sweet to Daddy.' Using the correct target utterance, the child must now be able to instruct you to act. Most children omit the preposition at first:
'Give (the) sweet Daddy.'
Keep modelling the correct form. Using a sign for 'to' greatly assists the hearing-impaired child.

Activity 2:

Target:
Pass/give it/(the) ball/bucket to me.

Materials:
A variety of objects.
Place the objects at a distance and take turns asking one another to:
'Pass the bucket to me.'
'Pass the bucket to her/him.'
If you are working with a group you may vary the pronoun.

Variation:
In order to emphasise the pronoun **it**, play with a construction kit (Lego, Montini) or do a puzzle.

Target:
Pass/give it (a piece of puzzle, a single block) to me/him/her.

Other examples of this structure used by children may include:

> He bought the girl a puppy.
> He gave the car a wash (a kick).
> I asked you a question.
> I'll tell you the secret.
> Mommy paid the man the money.
> You bring me the water.
> You do this to me.
> Mommy reads me the book.
> She shows him her car.
> I'll teach you the lesson.
> You throw me the ball.
> You find me an apple.
> Please make me a cake.
> (Quirk *et al.* 1972.)

Phrases

D Adj N: Determiner plus Adjective plus Noun:
The big car, this ugly cat.
(For Activities, see **Adj N** in Stage II. See also Book 3, The Determiner.)

Adj Adj N: Adjective plus Adjective plus Noun:
Big fat man, small red ball.

Use the activities described in Stage II (**Adj. N**). Introduce the second adjective by using appropriate objects or picture cards:
A big red ball, a small red ball, a dirty red ball, a clean red ball.
Numbers may be included: one red ball, two yellow balls.
(See Book 3, Adjectives.)

Prep Det N: Preposition plus Determiner plus Noun:
Under the table, with my friend.

Combine the activities described in Stage II for **Prep N** and **Det N**. Be sure the child does not omit either the preposition or the determiner.

Pronouns: Any items which can replace a Noun phrase. These can be personal or indefinite(s).

P Personal: I, you he etc.
O Other : This is mine
(See Book 3, The Pronoun.)

Cop (Copula): Refers to the verb to be, in any of its forms, when it is the only verb in a clause:
He **is** cross.
He **is** a clown.
(See Book 3, The Verb Phrase.)

Aux: Auxiliary verbs which alter the time, tense, and aspect of the main verb.
M Modal: **can/could** walk
O   **have been** sick. **do** come
(See Book 3, the Verb Phrase.)

6. Transition to Stage IV

Expansions

This section on the LARSP refers to phrase expansions only. The expansion of clauses occurs at Stage V.

XY + S:NP: A three-element Clause, with its Subject expanded by a Clause or Phrase:

The blue car(s) go fast.
The naughty boy(s) chase me.
The funny clown is happy.

Activities:

Insert any of the noun phrases already mastered into the Clauses SVC, SVO, SVA.

SVC:

Target:
The big/small girl/boy is happy/cross.
Use the activity described for SVC Stage III, but be sure your illustrations include: a big girl; a small girl; a big boy; a small boy – each one with a happy face; and identical cards – all with cross faces. This will ensure that the target utterance is achieved.

SVO:

Target:
This/that boy eats(s)/cut(s) apple(s)/banana(s).

Materials:
Two model boy dolls; a blunt knife; two apples; two bananas.
Place one boy (this boy) close to the child, and place the other at a distance (that boy). Discuss the action as you manipulate the toys appropriately:
'This boy cuts (the) apple.'
'This boy cuts (the) banana.'
or:
'This boy cuts apple(s) / that boy cuts banana(s)'.

SVA:

Target:
The red car/the blue car/the red lorry/the blue lorry go(es) fast/slow(ly)/down.

Materials:
A red car, a red truck, a blue car, a blue truck.
Using a sloping surface activate the model vehicles to race down the slope, and describe the activity appropriately:
'The red lorry goes fast.'
Now allow the child to activate the toy as you use the target, and vice versa.

XY + V:VP: A three-element Clause, with its Verb expanded by a Verb phrase:
I am jumping high.
Daddy can eat some.

Activities:

SVC:

Target:
He/she/they is/are being naughty/good.

Materials:
Doll family or puppets; water to splash or spill; crayons and paper. Activate the dolls to splash the water or scribble; wipe up the water or draw constructively. Encourage the child to describe the activity appropriately:
'He/she is being good/naughty.'

SVO:

Use the activities described for **SVO/** Stage III; vary the statement to incorporate the verb forms which the child has mastered:
Daddy is driving/drives/will drive the car.
The boy can ride the horse.
The boy wants to ride the horse.
(See Book 3, The Verb Phrase.)

SVA:

Target:
(The) elephant/giraffe/tiger/rhino will jump/come later.

Materials:
Model animals, a fenced enclosure.
Line the animals up, one behind the other. Activate each in turn to jump the fence or to walk into the enclosure. Point to the animal behind the moving one and say:
'The tiger will jump/come later.'
Be sure the child demonstrates an understanding of the concept by using the target utterance appropriately himself.

VCA:

Target:
Is being naughty/will be good now/later.
Use the activity for **SVC (V:VP)** but omit the subject, and use the adverbial: now/later.

VOA:

Target:
Don't put Mommy/Daddy there/here.
Don't put (the) car/lorry here/there.
Don't put the sheep/cow/pig here/there.

Materials:
Model vehicles, people and animals; model farm, house and garage or objects to represent these locations. Take turns in placing the animals, people and vehicles in the appropriate or inappropriate locations, aiming for the target utterance. For example, place a cow in the garage so that the child must tell you: 'Don't put the cow there!'

Note:
Although the **Neg V** only develops at Stage IV and the obligatory 'do' is difficult to master, children tend to learn 'don't' somewhat earlier – they are exposed to it so often.

VO$_d$O$_i$:

Target:
(I/you) want to give the ball/shoe to Mommy/Daddy.
It is impossible for you to use this structure without a subject. Use the activities described for **VO$_d$O$_i$** (Stage III) or **SVO$_d$O$_i$** (Stage IV) and the Verb Phrase in the target. The child may well omit the Subject, which is acceptable at this stage of his development.

XY + C:NP: A three-element Clause, with its Complement expanded by a Noun phrase or Clause and the remaining elements described as XY:
(The) clown is very cross.
(The) apple is not nice.

SVC:

Target:
Sugar/(a)lemon is nice/is not nice to eat.

Materials:
Some sugar, a lemon or any other foods.
Enjoy cutting and tasting the foods, encouraging the child to imitate your use of the target utterance:
'A lemon is not nice to eat.'

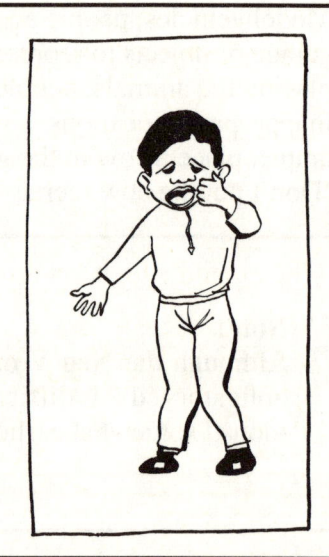

VCA:

Target:
Is cross again/is not cross now.

Materials:
Crayons and drawing paper.
Draw pictures of faces with various expressions – happy faces, cross faces, sad faces. Encourage the child to imitate your use of the target utterance:
'(He)'s not cross now, (the boy) is cross again.'
You must model **SVCA**, but the child may omit the subject.

XY + O:NP: A three-element Clause, with its Object expanded by a Noun Phrase or Clause, the remaining elements being referred to as **XY**:
Mommy, wash my face.
John, push the big wagon.

Activities:

SVO:

Target:
I/you wash/dry the baby('s) toes/eyes/nose.

Materials:
A doll and bath.
Bath the doll, encouraging the child to imitate your utterances:
'I wash the baby's nose. You dry the baby's toes.'
Use any of the other activities described for SVO (Stage III) making sure you expand the Objectival element to a Phrase or Clause.

VOA:

Target:
Make/build a high tower/ a long bridge/ a big house here/there.

Materials:
Blocks or crayons and drawing paper.
Instruct one another to:
'Build a high tower there. Make a long bridge here.'

VO$_d$O$_i$:

Target:
Give the big red car/ the small yellow car/the small red car/ the big yellow car to Mommy.

Materials:
A big red car; a small red car; a big yellow car; a small yellow car; model dolls.
Use the activities described for VO$_d$O$_i$ (Stage III), but be sure to expand the Direct Object. To **expand the Indirect Object**: use model animals and foods.

Target:
Give the bread/biscuit to the small brown dog/big black dog.

XY + A:AP: A three-element Clause with its Adverbial expanded by an Adverbial Phrase or Clause, the remaining elements referred to as XY:
Pour water in the bath.
Boy, go to school!
Lion, walk with the elephant.

SVA:

Target:
(The) lion/elephant/giraffe stand(s)/lies/walk(s) in front of/behind/by the jeep/lorry/car.
(The selection of vehicles to be used in the Adverbial Phrase is made deliberately, as these are objects with a clear front and back, making the cognition of the words 'behind' and 'in front' more meaningful.)

Materials:
Model animals and vehicles as listed in the target.
Model trees or a picture of the countryside may help to set a game reserve scene.
Using a single subject, an elephant, place it behind the jeep, lorry or car:
'(The) elephant stand(s) behind (the) jeep.'
When the child has mastered this target by responding correctly to your statement and by using the target appropriately, increase the complexity by varying first the subject:
'(The) elephant/giraffe/lion stands in front of the jeep.'
Then the verb:
'The elephant/giraffe/lion stands/lies/walks in front of (the) jeep.'
Finally, if the child is able to cope with this step, vary the preposition within the adverbial phrase:
'The elephant/giraffe/lion stands/walks/lies in front of/behind/by (the) jeep/car/lorry.'

Variation 1:

Target:
Boy/Girl/Mommy go to the bathroom/kitchen/lounge!

Materials:
Model doll family, a doll's house or picture cards depicting the rooms of the house.
Activate the dolls appropriately and allow the child using the target utterances to do so:
'Mommy, go to the bathroom.'
'Daddy, go to the lounge.'

Variation 2:

Target:
Mommy/Daddy/Boy/Girl go to the shop/ to school/to work.

Materials:
Model doll family; model buildings or pictures depicting a school, a shop etc.

Variation 3:
Instruct one another:
'You (Kenny) go to the window/door.'

VOA:

Target:
Put/hide (the) book/pen/ball under/on/in/behind (the) box/cupboard.

Materials:
A book, a pen, a ball, a box, the cupboard in your room.
Using a single Object at first, instruct one another to:
'Hide the book in the cupboard/box.'
Then vary the Object:
'Hide the book/pen/ball under the box/cupboard.'
Vary your use of Verbs:
'Hide/put the book/pen/ball in the cupboard/box.'
Finally vary the Preposition:
'Hide/put the book/pen/ball behind/in/under the box/cupboard.'
If there are more than two 'players' the third may leave the room while the other two instruct one another to 'hide the ball under the box'. The third must then hunt for it.

Variation:
Pour the juice in the cup.
Pour the water in the bath.
Pour the water on the flowers.
Pour the milk in the baby's bottle.

Materials:
Water, milk, juice, a variety of appropriate objects. Instruct one another to pour the liquids into or onto the appropriate containers and objects. Then have some fun pouring the liquids into or onto the inappropriate objects:
'Pour the milk in the bath.'
'Pour the juice on the flowers.'
Children should learn to play with words in this manner.

VCA:

Target:
Is (a) cat like yours.

Materials:
Crayons and drawing paper, or a duplicate set of model animals. Assist the child to draw or select an animal, then draw or select the same animal using the target:

'It(s) a cat like yours.'

Note the inclusion of the subject **it** making this utterance grammatically correct. The child may either omit the subject or the verb:

'It a cat like yours – is a cat like yours.'

This is developmentally appropriate.

7. Stage IV

Remember, more than one element may now be expanded.

Clauses

Commands

+ S: A command with the Subject expressed. Utterances may have one or several other clause elements:
'You, come here!'
'All the boys, sit down now!'

Activities:

Select any Command from Stages II, III or IV and attach an expressed Subject to these:

VO_dO_i: Give the ball to Mommy.
Now, precede the utterance thus:
'You/Daniel, give the ball to Mommy!'

VOA:
Put your cars on the table.

Target:
All the boys, put your cars on the table.
All the girls, put your balls in the box.

Materials:
Several boy and girl model dolls, balls and model cars.
(See activities for VO_dO_i and VOA - Stage III.)

VXY +: A Command verb with two or more elements following:
Give me the keys quickly.
Put the big ball in the yellow box.
(See all previous structures commencing with a verb.)

Questions

QVS: A question word plus Subject–Verb inversion:
Where is it?
What's it for?
(See Book 3, Questions.)

QXY +: A question word accompanied by two other clause elements, but without the inversions required in mature speech. The plus sign indicates any further elements:
What you are doing with that baby?
Note: This inability to invert the verb is a normal developmental phenomenon. You must continue to model the correct form for the child.

VS (X +): A Subject/Verb inversion followed by more than one other element of clause structure:
Have you got a sweet?
(See Book 3, Verb and Question Forms.)

tag: A Verb plus Subject construction 'tagged' on to the main clause:
He wants it, doesn't he?
She's pretty, isn't she?

Introduce this in your story-telling – it is a device which encourages discourse. Tag questions are particularly interesting developments in child language as they involve management of pronouns, auxiliary verbs and rules for verb inversion. For more detail on this particular structure, the reader is referred to Slobin (1967).

Statements

SVOA: Subject plus Verb plus Object plus Adverbial:
I will put the ball here.
Mommy drives her car to the shop.
(See Stage III – **SVO** and expansion of **S,V,O & A**.)

Activity 1:

Target:
Mommy/daddy drives the car/lorry to the shop/to work/ round the corner/on the road very fast/slowly.

Materials:
A map depicting roads and buildings (see Book 1, Equipment); model dolls and vehicles.
The child activates the models on the map while describing where and how they are moving:
'Mommy drives the car fast.'
'Daddy drives the lorry to work.'
Take turns in activating the toys while the other 'player' closes his eyes and tries to guess the action.

Activity 2:

Target:
The boy/farmer drives/pushes/rides the horse/cow/pig into/behind/in front of the barn.

Materials:
Model farm animals and model dolls.
Repeat the activity as in Activity 1.

Activity 3:

Target:
I want the ball/tractor/fish now.

Materials:
A variety of attractive toys placed in a container.
Using the target utterance, take turns in using the utterance to retrieve a toy.

Activity 4:

Target:
You put the dog/pig/horse/that piece (of puzzle) here/there.

Materials:
A puzzle, model farmyard animals.
Alternatively instruct one another:
'You put that piece (of puzzle) here.'
or
'You put the cow there.'

Activity 5:

Target:
I'm going to draw/drew toes/eyebrows on the foot/face.

Materials:
Paper and crayons.

Activity:
Take turns drawing parts of the body in the appropriate places on an outlined figure. Encourage the child to use the target utterance:
'I'm going to draw/ I'll draw/I drew a nose/eyebrows on the face.'
You may draw body parts on the incorrect appendages to add a fun element.
'I'll draw the toes on the hands!'

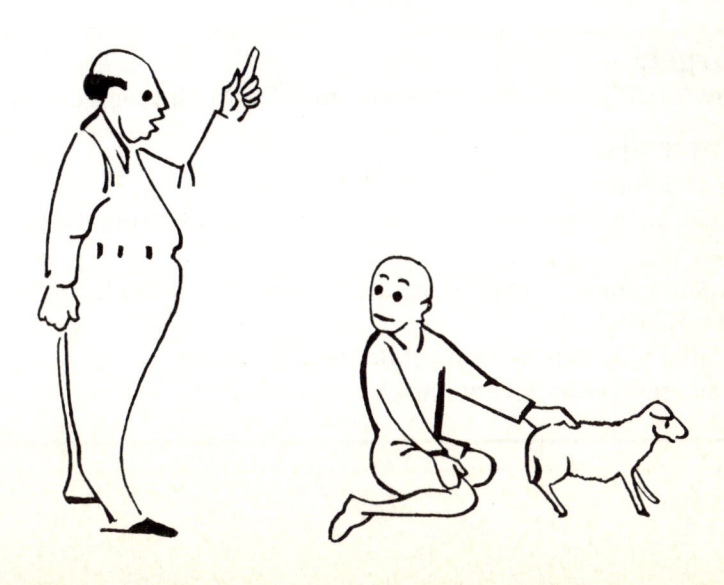

SVCA: Subject plus Verb plus Complement plus Adverbial:
The girl was happy then.
He was a fireman long ago.
(See **SVC** - Stage III and any Subject, Verb, Complement or Adverbial expansions.)

Activity 1:

Target:
The man/boy/girl is happy/sad/cross now.

Materials:
Crayons and drawing paper; a mask-face without features; cut-out shapes of eyes, nose and mouth.
Make several 'mouths' – some smiling, some drooping. Cut-out 'tears' will add to the effect!
(a) Draw faces depicting varied emotions and use the target utterance to describe these:
'He is smiling now.'
'He is sad now.'
(b) Use the mask and cut-outs to depict changing emotions. Make sure the child has a turn to draw and describe.

Activity 2:

Target:
Now/first/then the tower/train is small/big/high/long/gets bigger.

Materials:
Wooden blocks.
Construct a block tower or train with the child, using the target utterance:
'First the train is small. Now the train is long. Then the tower gets bigger.'
Parallel play may spur the child on to compete:
'Now my tower is very high.'

SVO$_d$O$_i$: Subject plus Verb plus Direct and Indirect Objects:
He gives her a book.
They gave their coats to the children.
(See **VO$_d$O$_i$** – Stage III and any Verb or Object expansions.)

Introduce a subject by using one of the model dolls or a member of your group as an actor:

'Mommy gives the ball to the boy.'

Variations:

Target:
I'll give the ball/shoe to Mommy/Ralph.
The child shares out the objects amongst the model dolls or group members. Be sure to ask him first:
'What will you give to Mommy?'
For the purposes of this exercise encourage a full rather than an elliptical response. In regular discourse the answer would simply be:
'Ball!'

Activity:
The child shares out the objects to the group or model dolls. Close your eyes and guess:
'Did you give the ball to Daddy?'
If your guess is incorrect, encourage him to tell you:
'I gave the ball to Mommy.'
Reverse roles if he is able to ask the question.
(See Book 3, Questions.)

SVOC: Subject plus Verb plus Object plus Complement.
I'll make it a snake.
He called me a fool.
She made me sad.
(See **SVC** – Stage III and any Subject, Verb, Object or Complement expansions.)

Activity 1:

Target:
He/she made the boy/girl/them sad/happy/cross/angry.

Materials:
Picture cards depicting the following: a mother giving a child a smack or, alternatively, a sweet; a woman looking angry as a dog with muddy paws soils the carpet etc.
Assist the child to describe the pictures appropriately:
'Mommy made the girl sad.'
'The dog made Mommy cross.'
(These materials may be used to teach the Conjunction 'because' – see Book 3, Conjunctions.)

Activity 2:

Target:
'I'll make it a snake/a basket/a rope.'

Materials:
Playdough or plasticine.
While modelling objects such as those listed in the target, encourage the child to use the appropriate utterances:
'I'll make it/this a snake.'

Variation:
Draw a man, adding the appropriate and characteristic features:
'I'll make him a policeman.'

AAXY: Two Adverbials and any two elements of Clause structure, labelled **X** and **Y** respectively:

I'm going to school tomorrow.
I came to your house with my swimming costume.
They went there quickly.
The cow walks slowly after the man.
Throw the ball far over there.
Put the ball here, under the table.

Activity 1:

Target:
Put the ball/car here/there under the table/on the table.
or
Put the ball under/on here/there (indicating location).

Materials:
A selection of objects and localities (a table, a chair).
Take turns in placing the objects according to one another's instructions:
'Put the ball there, under the table.'

Activity 2:

Target:
The cow/horse/pig walks slowly/fast after/behind/with/to the duck/sheep/donkey.
Take turns in manipulating the animals while describing their actions:
'The cow walks slowly behind the pig.'
Be sure to vary one element at a time if the child finds the target too complex. For example you may use only two animals, or you may select a single preposition **behind** to begin with.

Phrases

NP Pr NP: Noun Phrase plus Preposition plus Noun Phrase:

The boy with the dog.
The lady in a coat.
The ball under the table.
(See **Pr N** – Stage II and all expansions of the Noun Phrase).

Activity 1:

Target:
The boy/girl/man with a coat/hat/umbrella.

Materials:
Picture cards illustrating all the variables (as described in the target): a boy with a hat; a boy with a coat etc.
Keeping the subject constant, place all the pictures of boys face downwards. Take turns guessing which boy/garment combination it will be before turning up the card:
'The boy with the coat!'
Caution: Do not extend the utterance at this stage:
'This is the boy with the coat.'

Variation:

Target:
A ball/car under/on/behind the table/chair bed.

Materials:
Picture cards depicting the target utterances as in Activity 1:
A ball under a table; a ball on a table; a ball under a chair etc. Use the cards as in Activity 1.

Pr D Adj N: Preposition plus Determiner plus Adjective plus Noun:
Behind the big car.
In the red basket.

Activities:
See **D Adj N** and **Prepositions** (Book 3). Make sure to use a variety of adjectives, determiners, prepositions and nouns contrasting a single grammatical form at a time:

Targets:
In/on/behind the red basket.
In this/that/those/these red basket(s).
In the red/yellow/blue basket.
In the red basket/box.

---

cX: Any phrasal construction introduced by a Co-ordinating Conjunction (**c**), usually **and**:

And you; and the lion.

Although children may use this structure, the model given by you may be **XcX** - two phrasal constructions linked by a co-ordinating conjunction, usually **and**:

Boy and girl.
You and me.
A big dog and a small dog.

Activity 1:

Target:
You/her and me/him.
or
Yours/hers and mine/his.

Materials:
Any tokens to be shared, or an activity requiring turn taking. Model dolls can be used as the other participants if you are not working with a group.
Sit close to the child, indicating that you are partners. Place the dolls or other participants together at some distance from the two of you. Now proceed to share out the tokens or take turns in the game, saying:
'(One is) yours and mine, (one is) his and hers, (a turn for) you and me, (a turn for) him and her.'

Activity 2:

Target:
Daddy and Mommy and the girl...
The cow and the pig and the sheep.

Materials:
Model dolls and animals.
Place the dolls or animals in the child's hand, one by one, whilst you enumerate:
'The cow and the pig and the sheep.'
Be sure to stress the conjunction **and**. Now encourage the child to give you the models but do not accept them if he omits to say 'and'.

Variation:

Target:
The ball or the car.
Using the conjunction **or**, present the child with two attractive objects, allowing him to select one:
'(Do you want) the ball or the car?'
Reverse roles so that he uses the target utterance while offering you a choice.

Neg V: A Negative word within the Verb Phrase – as opposed to its earlier status as a particle external to clause structure:
He is not coming.
She is not good.
(See Book 3, Verbs and the Negative.)

The development of the grammatically correct form of verb negative depends entirely on the development of the auxiliary, and hence does not occur until this stage. The process of negation within the sentence involves the insertion and correct placement of a negative word.

Neg X: A Negative word within a Phrase other than the Verb Phrase:
He's four, not five (years old).
(See Book 3, Negative.)

2 Aux: Any sequence of two Auxiliary Verbs within the Verb Phrase:
He will be coming.
She does have to go.
(See Book 3, Verbs.)

8. Stage V

(See also Book 3, Conjunctions and Personal Pronouns.)

Clauses

In this stage, complex sentence formation emerges as clauses are strung together or embedded one in another. There are four types of connectives recorded on the LARSP. **And** is noted separately as it is the most frequently used connective. Other co-ordinations (**c**) are grouped together – for example, **or** and **but**. Subordinating conjunctions such as **when**, **although**, **because** and **which**, are also grouped under a separate category – (**s**).

Two main classes of clausal connection are noted on the LARSP – namely Co-ordination (**Coord**) and Subordination (**Subord**).

> **Coord 1**: Two Clauses linked by **and** or (**c**) :
> The man caught a rabbit and the boy caught a bird.
> Go outside but don't slip in the mud.
> **Coord 1+**: More than two Clauses linked by **and** or (**c**):
> I went home and I swam and I ate my lunch.
> Go to the kitchen and bring me water but don't hurry.
> **Subord A1:** A Clause containing an Adverbial element which is also a Clause:
> He came when I called him.
> **Subord A1+**: A Clause containing at least two Adverbial Clauses:
> The man drove when it was late because his car had a flat tyre.
>
> **Subord s:** A clause containing a Subjectival (s) element which is itself a clause:
> What she did made me cross.
> **Subord c:** A clause containing a Complement (c) element which is itself a clause:
> This is what I need.
> **Subord o:** A clause containing an Object (o) element which is itself a clause:
> He saw what I meant.
> **Comparative**: A clause containing a grammatical marker of comparison: It is **higher than** that.

Note: Pink and Thomas (1970) classify this as an Adverbial Clause.

Adverbial clauses are classified semantically by Pink and Thomas (1970).

1) **Time**: He came after I left.
The conjunctions introducing time clauses include: after; as; before; till; until; when (ever); while; since.
2) **Place**: I'll follow wherever you go.
3) **Cause**: The boy cried because he fell.
4) **Purpose**: He worked hard so he would pass.
5) **Result**: He worked so hard that he became ill.
6) **Condition**: I'll come if you're good.
7) **Concession**: Even if you're there, I won't do it.

Questions and Commands:

These also include co-ordination as described above.

Question Coord: When did he go and why didn't he come back?
Question Other: What did you do before you came here?
Command Coord: Be quiet and don't talk!
Command Other: Come home when you are finished!

Crystal (1982) notes that co-ordination emerges before subordination in the child with normally developing language.

Phrases

A few clauses may also be seen as part of noun–phrase structure, as a means of modifying the head noun, and may occur once or several times.

Postmodifying clause: :
1: The boy who came here is gone.
1+: That's the ball which you threw and which popped.
(See Book 3, Personal Pronouns.)

Postmodifying phrase:
1+: the man in the train with the dog.
(A simple postmodifying phrase is the same structure as **NP Pr NP** (above).
Note: for activities to teach Co-ordination, Subordination and Post-modifying Clauses and Phrases, see Book 3, Personal Pronouns and Conjunctions.

Word

This column refers to the use of inflectional endings affecting morphological structure. These word endings with a grammatical function begin to emerge from the beginning of Stage II.

ing: As in **aux + ing**:
Eating, sitting.
(See Book 3, Verb Forms.)

pl: Any plural form, regular or irregular.
Care should be taken to introduce the regular form first.

Activity:

Target:
A/the/ball/car – some/lots of/two/more balls/cars.

Materials:
Several model cars and balls.
Using the appropriate Determiners, ask the child to give you:
'One ball, some cars.'
Reverse roles.
(See Book 3, Indefinite Pronouns or Noun Modifiers.)

-ed: Single past tense form, whether regular or irregular:
Walked, ran.
(For Activities, see Book 3, Verbs.)

-en: Past participle form, whether regular or irregular.
I have taken/It's broken/He has been going.
(See Book 3, Verb Forms.)

3s: Third person singular present tense form, whether regular or irregular:
He walks, goes, is, has.

Activity:

Target:
A zebra/giraffe/camel runs/sleeps/walks.
Zebras/giraffes/camels walk/run/sleep.

Materials:
Pictures or models depicting agents and actors listed in the target. Allow the child to select the appropriate stimulus as you model the target utterance: a picture of two zebras running and a picture of one zebra running.
You say:
'The zebras run.'
The child places a token on the appropriate picture. Then encourage the child to describe the contrasting pictures appropriately.

---

gen: Genitive form of a noun – regular or irregular.
Boy's cars, men's hats, cats' whiskers, girls' dresses.

This is a natural extension of the work on **NN** (Phrase Stage II) described earlier. Use the activities described, but now do not accept the child's utterance as correct unless he uses the genitive form.

Note: Hearing-impaired children will have great difficulty perceiving this structure. The use of manual codes may be of assistance here.

n't: The contracted negative form:
Can't, doesn't, won't.
Children must be encouraged to use these forms rather than the more formal structures – cannot, does not, will not – as they are more appropriate in discourse.
(See Book 3, The Negative.)

'cop: The contracted form of the copula verb:
He's good, it's a monkey.

'aux: The contracted form of the auxiliary verb:
He's running, I'm sitting, you're hopping.

Both **'cop** and **'aux** should be encouraged when used in the appropriate context.
(See Book 3, Verb Forms.)

-est: The superlative form of an adjective or adverb, whether regular or irregular:
Biggest, strongest, best.

-er: The comparative form of an adjective or adverb, whether regular or irregular:
Bigger, stronger, better.

Activities:

Target:
Daddy/Mommy/the girl/the boy/the baby is taller/shorter than...
He/she is the tallest/shortest.

Materials:
Cut-out dolls depicting a family, ranging in appropriate sizes from tallest to shortest.
(See Book 3, Adverbs.)
Assist the child to place the cut-outs in order of size while you question or command:
'Who is the tallest? Give me the shortest.'
Now select only two dolls to demonstrate comparison:
'Which one is taller/shorter?'

Variations:
Use graded sized animals or objects to depict big, bigger, biggest; ladders or block towers of varying height for high, higher and highest.
Draw stick figures to depict fat, fatter, fattest or thin, thinner, thinnest.
Use lengths of string for long, longer, longest and short, shorter, shortest.
Use bean bags for heavy, heavier, heaviest and light, lighter, lightest;
and percussion instruments for loud, louder, loudest, soft softer, softest.

-ly: The ending used to mark an adverb word class: quickly, slowly.

Activity:

Targets:
Walk/run quickly/slowly.
Pack (them) tidily/untidily.
Play/beat the drum/speak loudly/softly/ quietly.
Draw/colour in nicely.

Materials:
Objects to be packed into a container; musical instruments; drawing materials.
The child acts out the appropriate instructions:
'Walk quickly, speak quietly, draw nicely, pack them away quickly!'
Reverse roles so that he uses the target utterances and you act out his instructions. Include a naughty puppet who will not obey instructions. This gives you the opportunity to introduce opposites and the negative. Instruct the puppet to 'colour in nicely'. When he has scribbled over the lines, discuss this with the child:
'Did he do it nicely? No, he didn't. He worked untidily.'

9. Stage VI

'Two distinct processes seem to be operating [at this stage]' (Crystal 1982).

(+) implies new types of construction.
(-) these are errors made on all previous constructions.

+

NP: Noun Phrase.

Initiator: This refers to items preceding the determiner in a noun phrase:
All the boys, both the men.
(See Book 3, Indefinite Pronouns or Noun Modifiers.)

Coord: This refers to cases where two noun phrases are co-ordinated without any formal marker of co-ordination present:
Jack, the baker.
See the birdie, a canary.

> ### Activity:
> This is best modelled in a story sequence by giving as many examples of this structure as are relevant within a single narrative.

VP: Verb Phrase.

Complex: This applies to verb phrases where more than one component of the verb appears. Whereas the simple auxiliary emerges at Stage 3, the later-developing ones (coded as **2 AUX** on the LARSP chart) contain two components, for example:

>He might have run.

Complex verb forms include three-part auxiliaries (for example: He might have been running) and other aspects discussed later in Book 3. Crystal (1982) gives the example:

>He might not go.

This contains an auxiliary and a negative.
(See Book 3, Verb Forms.)

Passive:

Clause:

The man was bitten by the dog.
The bike was ridden by the boy.

Activity:

Targets:
The bike/horse was ridden by the boy.
The man was bitten by the dog/snake/lion.
The apple/banana was eaten by the girl.
The ball was thrown/kicked by the man.

Materials:
Models of all the items listed in the targets.
Activate each subject and object appropriately while modelling the target utterance. Using the following techniques, assist the child to use the appropriate structures:
(a) Forced alternative:
'Is/was the apple eaten by the girl or is/was the banana eaten by the boy.'
(b) Use of the ridiculous: Interchange the subject and object:
'The boy is bitten by the dog.'
'The dog is bitten by the boy.'
(c) Commence the utterance, allowing the child to complete it:
'The apple...'
'The horse....'

Complement:

He is loath to do it.
I'm good at maths.

Activities:

These structures will appear in narration and discourse and must be taught by this means.

How/What:

These are clauses with exclamatory function, denoted by the use of question words. Note there is no reversal of subject and verb, as in the question form. These stylistic clauses may also be learned in discourse. Teaching basic grammatical structures is essential, but conversational style allows the child to use his language in varying social contexts, and should be learned within such contexts:

> How big it is!
> What a good boy you are!

(-)

This section on the LARSP refers to mistakes made by children in the process of mastering linguistic rules. It is most important to acknowledge that these are logical steps which occur during the language learning process. They indicate progress as the child internalises rules and rule exceptions. A typical example of such rule generalisation is that of regular to irregular past tense. Many children generalise the regular form, and will use such structures as 'I goed' or 'I drinked' before mastering the irregular forms 'went' and 'drank'.

A number of these features have been found to be characteristic of non-standard English in South Africa and, as such, should not be remediated even at later stages.

The LARSP enumerates the types of developmental errors which require correction only at the appropriate stages of development, when these should already have been mastered by the child.

It is important to heed Crystal's warning that one should not automatically assume that an incorrect form constitutes an error. It is an indicator of a naturally emerging structure.

Conn:

Connectivity. This refers to the main types of problems displayed during the learning of connecting words:
and: used instead of a more appropriate marker:

> He broke his leg **and** he fell off his bike.
> **c**: He broke his leg **so** the bike fell.
> **s**: The bike fell **because** he broke his arm.

Clause:

Element Ø: Element omitted:
He put on chair (Object omitted).
Mommy ball (Verb omitted).

⇌ Element order reversed:
The car the man drive (OSV where SVO is the target).

Concord: The subject does not agree in number with another element:

I are going.
He jump.

Phrase:

NP Noun Phrase.
D: The wrong form of determiner:
This hats.
DØ : omission of determiner:
I want _____ ball.
D⇌ : The determiner is incorrectly placed:
Ball **this** here.
Pr: The incorrect preposition is selected:
Put the book **in** the table.
PrØ: omission of preposition:
Put the book _____ table.
Pr⇌ : The preposition is in the wrong place:
Put the book table **on**.
Pron [p]: Any error in the use of personal pronouns:
Him a good boy.
His dress (referring to a girl).

VP: Verb Phrase
Aux [m]: Any error in the use of modal Auxiliaries whether of substitution or word order:
She **jump** can't.
She **can** jump. (implying the imperative 'must').
Aux [o]: Any errors in the use of other auxiliaries whether of substitution or word order:
She **be** sitting.
She going **be**.

143

Aux Ø: omissions of any auxiliary:
She_____coming.
Cop: All copula errors:
He_____naughty.
She be happy

Word

This refers to errors in inflectional endings used in the structures described under **Words** earlier in the chart.

> **N irreg**: The wrong form of an irregular noun: **mices**.
> **V irreg**: The wrong form of an irregular verb: **goed**, **ated**.
> **N reg**: The wrong form of a regular noun: **catses**.
> **V reg**: The wrong form of a regular verb: **I hoppen** (hopped).

The development of discourse skills and comprehension skills at Stage VII of the LARSP profile will not be delineated in this text. Once the child has progressed to Stage VI and is using complex sentences, once he has a large vocabulary and has established a good pragmatic repertoire, language therapy moves from a consideration of structure to the areas of content and use. At this stage there should be an overlap with the language skills taught in the school curriculum, with emphasis on the development of text, on rules of linking sentences, and on conversational competence. These topics deserve a book in themselves and cannot be dealt with here as our focus is on the earliest stages of developing language competence.

BOOK THREE

Therapy with special grammatical categories – the phrasal component

Introduction

Having considered some therapy suggestions for each of the stages of LARSP, we are now going to consider therapy with some special grammatical categories. These have been selected as the most commonly affected categories in the language-impaired child. These include:

    Determiners
    Pronouns
    Verbs
    Negatives
    Questions
    Conjunctions
    Adverbs
    Adjectives
    Prepositions

As we have seen, the first five of these categories have been considered by Laura Lee in her evaluation and remediation of syntax – the programme known as Developmental Sentence Analysis, which involves a developmental progression for each structure. The first three sections have been included here for their considered clinical relevance. The verb section in particular has been developed at length since it acts as an extension for the advanced stages in LARSP, which are often a puzzle to clinicians. Furthermore, verbs are the essential basis for the development of questions and negatives. See Table 3 for the order of acquisition of grammatical forms (Lee 1974).

The development of adverbs and adjectives in a child's repertoire may be considered the 'cherry on the top', but it is nevertheless an essential component of further language development. We have found that many clinical children have impoverished descriptive language, and we therefore believe that at school level, adverbial and adjectival activities would also be of considerable advantage in developing other language skills.

1. Determiners

Determiners occur before a noun. They specify the range of reference of that noun in various ways: by making the noun definite (the boy); indefinite (a boy); or by indicating quantity (many boys). The choice of determiner is influenced by the class of noun.

The most important category of determiner is the central determiner, which includes articles, demonstratives, possessives and quantifiers. The category includes words such as a, an, this, these, that, those, my, your, some, any, every. Determiners resemble attributive, premodifying adjectives.

The article: the, a(n)

The article belongs to the determiner class. Articles generally appear before common or count nouns in the noun phrase (a book, the boys), and they do not have any function independent of the noun which they precede. They contribute definite or indefinite status to the noun which they determine. New information tends to be presented by definite articles.

The acquisition of definiteness (the book) and indefiniteness (a book) has been studied extensively. Studies have shown that children of three years of age are able to make correct use of the definite article 'to make referents that are uniquely given in previous discourse. It is not clear, however, that the children were only reacting to this dimension of the use of articles' (Romaine 1984, p. 143).

Karmiloff (cited by Romaine 1984) argues, however, that three- and four-year-old children use the indefinite article for deixis, often accompanied by pointing. She states that determiners are multi-functional and that children only acquire full control over them at the age of ten.

Language-deviant and language-delayed children tend to omit the article, since it carries less meaning than other structures in the sentence. Hearing-impaired children may have difficulty hearing **the** and **a**, as these syntactical structures are usually unstressed.

There are two ways to introduce the article, but it seems that for its use to become habitual, constant reminding, and non-response on the part of the listener when it has been omitted, are the only ways of encouraging the child to include it.

The most useful techniques for eliciting this structure include imitation, pointing out the error, corrective levels, silence!, and the use of manual coding (see Book One, Techniques).

Activities to teach the article need to demonstrate the meaning of definiteness/indefiniteness, and may also serve to contrast demonstratives.

Activity 1:

Target:
The, a, an.

Materials:
Smarties or raisins, coloured boxes or Tupperware blocks (three red and three yellow containers).
First place a single red container and a single yellow container on the table. The child hides the sweet in one of the containers. You guess:
'(In) the red one.'
When you make the correct choice, the sweet is yours. Reverse roles and ensure that the child uses the target **the** in the noun phrase.
Now add the other containers – you have three red and three yellow boxes. Repeat the activity, using the relevant indefinite article: '(In) a yellow box?'
When you have selected the correct colour, point to each box in turn and say:
'In this box?'
When you have finally guessed correctly, it is the child's turn to find the hidden sweet.

Activity 2:

Target:
The, a, an.

Materials:
Models: Two red aeroplanes, two blue aeroplanes, two red cars, two blue cars, two red boats, two blue boats.
Using only a single car, boat and aeroplane at first, allow the child to hide one under a cloth. You guess which model has been hidden: 'The aeroplane? The car?'
Reverse roles.
Now use: one red and one blue car, one red and one blue aeroplane, one red boat and one blue boat. The target still remains the definite article **the**, and it is important for the child to understand why this is so, even with the added variable of colour.
Finally, use all the materials. As there are now two identical articles of the same colour, the indefinite factor is introduced and the child must use the appropriate article:
'A red car?'

Activity 3:

Target:
The, a, an.

Materials:
Well-illustrated books or sequence pictures of *Goldilocks and the Three Bears* and *The Three Little Pigs*. These stories offer much opportunity to use the target structures:
A girl named Goldilocks.
A daddy bear.
The porridge was hot.
The small chair.
A big/a small and a medium sized bed etc.
Three pigs – this one and that one.
A man with bricks.
A straw house.
A bad wolf.
Narrate the story and encourage the child to do so too. Using such techniques as completion, forced alternative and modelling (see Book One, Techniques), the child will be encouraged to use the correct noun phrase.

2. Pronouns

Pronouns 'replace' nouns or whole noun phrases. There are many different types of pronouns, but they have been divided by Lee into two grammatical categories, namely the indefinite pronouns and the personal pronouns.

Indefinite pronouns

Persons or things are mentioned without actually naming them (Pink and Thomas 1970). The indefinite pronoun may replace a determiner (D) or serve as one.

1) Demonstrative pronouns

Pink and Thomas (1970) and Lee (1974) classify these as indefinite pronouns, whilst Quirk *et al.* (1972) do not. Demonstrative (or deictic) pronouns indicate or 'point out' the person or thing to which they refer: **this/that**. (Lee has placed **these** and **those** in the column designated personal pronouns, although she acknowledges that they may be classified as indefinite pronouns – this arbitrary classification was made for the purpose of sentence scoring.) Such pronouns have 'near' reference – this/ these, and 'far' reference – that/those (Quirk *et al.*, 1972).

2) Pronouns of number (count)

These may either be positive or negative: somebody/nobody.

Positive pronouns may be ***universal***: each, all.

*****assertive***: one (day), some.

*****non-assertive***: either, any.

*****negative***: neither, nobody.

Activities for teaching indefinite pronouns

it

Used to describe only the subject of the sentence by the young child (Lee 1974).

Activity 1:
Materials:
A bag or pillowcase containing several large objects which the child is able to identify and name.
Allow the child to feel the objects in the bag without seeing them.
Ask:
'What is it?'
before he withdraws the article from the container and names it:
'It's a dog!'
Encourage him to ask the question and to supply the answer.

Note:
This activity may be combined with the negative target:
'It's not a dog.'
You make incorrect guesses about the identity of the object:
'It's a horse!'
Let him correct you:
'No it's not. It's a dog!'

Activity 2:
Materials:
Pictures of objects the child is able to identify and name.
Discuss and name the pictures, then turn them face downwards.
Take turns in picking up a picture as you ask of one another:
'What is it? (Is it) a ball?'
The response must incorporate the target:
'It's a car'.

Variation:
For the older child, use the picture cards as in a card game. Deal them out. Each 'player' holds up a card, the picture concealed from the opponent. The latter then guesses:
'It's a ball!'
If he is correct, he keeps the card.

Activity 3:
Materials:
Several objects.
Demonstrate by holding up a single object and describing it:
'It's got wheels. It's got four doors. It's.....a car!'
Now repeat the activity, but this time conceal the object and do not name it. Reverse roles, so that using the target utterance himself the child himself describes an object.

Activity 4:
Materials:
Coloured tokens.
Each 'player' has three different coloured tokens. Take turns hiding one token behind your back, while the other one guesses:
'Is it red?'
(See also Negative, and Question Reversals, below.)

Activity 5:
Target:
It.
Used in expressions of time, distance, weather, temperature and tide (Pink and Thomas 1970).
Materials:
Weather chart, a large clock.
Point to illustrations of climatic conditions on the chart, or set the time by adjusting the hands of the clock:
'Is it cold? No it's hot.'
'It's late. It's four o'clock.'
(See also Negative, and Question Reversals.)

this/that

These are indefinite pronouns:
>   This is mine.
>   That is yours.

They may also be used as determiners:
>   This tree is tall.
>   That book is torn.

Remember to maintain distance perspectives in these activities, and be sure to keep in close proximity to the child so that you maintain the same frame of reference.

Activity 1:

Materials:
Pairs of identical objects – blocks, model cars etc., matching picture cards.
Place one of each pair in front of you, and place the other some distance away. Command the child:
'(Give me) this/that (car).'
Remember to indicate non-verbally which object you are referring to. Allow the child to 'post' the object in a container so as to motivate him. Allow the child to command you using the relevant target. He may omit the verb and subject, using only the noun phrase:
'This/that car/block.'

Variation:

Using only model vehicles, the target becomes:
(Push) that/this car/bus/bike.
The forced alternative is a particularly useful technique for eliciting this structure:
'This car or that car?'

Activity 2:
Point to parts of your body or clothing and say:
'This (is my) nose.'
'This (is my) dress.'
Now point to the child:
'That('s your) nose.'
'That('s your) dress.'
When he attempts to imitate you, he may only be able to say:
'That/this nose/dress',
omitting the verb and determiner.

No, some, more, all, lot(s), one(s), two, other, another

(No – see no one, nobody, nothing, none, below)

Some

May be used as either a pronoun or a determiner, and may appear before plural or uncountable (mass) nouns (Lee 1974, Pink and Thomas 1970).

Activity:
Materials:
Marbles or tokens, a jug of water, empty cups.
Share out the objects, using the pronouns listed above:
Give me one.
Some are yours.
I want more.
All are in.
I want lot(s).
Two more!
Give me the other/another.
Pour the water into the cups using appropriate pronouns:
More!
Some!
All!
Lot(s).
It may be necessary to select one pronoun at a time until the child is familiar with its cognitive implication and has learnt to use it appropriately. He may use these pronouns as a single element at this stage:
More!
Some!

Something, somebody, someone

These compounds follow the same structural format as **some**.

Activity 1:

Target:
Somebody/someone.

Materials:
Model doll family.
Hide each doll in turn in a container. Say:
'Somebody/someone is in(side). Who (is it)?'
Encourage the child to guess.

Variations:
Use the question form:
'Is it Mummy?'
The negative:
'No it's not.'
(See also Negative and Questions.)
Also contrast with **nobody** by producing an empty container. Be sure that the child gets to use the target **somebody/someone**, **nobody/no one**.

Activity 2:

Target:
Something/nothing.

Materials:
Substitute model animals or objects for the doll family used in Activity 1.
Repeat the game, contrasting **something** with **nothing**.

Variation:
Make the appropriate sound as you place one animal or object in the box. Say:
'Something is barking/mewing. What (is it)?'
Allow the child to guess. Reverse roles. He may make the appropriate sound and use the single element pronoun in order to question you:
'Something?'

Nothing, nobody, no one

(See activities for Something/somebody/someone.)

None

Activity:

Materials:
Use mass (or uncountable) nouns – water, sand.
Pour the water or sand in and out of a container and describe:
'Look. None!' (contrast with **some**).

Any, anything, anybody, anyone

Any, like some, may be used as either a pronoun or adjective, and may appear before plural or mass nouns (Quirk *et al.* 1972).

Activity 1:

Target:
Any.

Materials:
Model cars; balls, marbles; sweets, apples; shoes. Pictures depicting: cars, balls, marbles, sweets, apples, shoes, bananas, buses, planes, socks.
Give all the objects to the child. Keep the pictures yourself. Hold up a picture and ask:
'(Do you have) any?'
Allow the child to match his objects with the picture. Reverse roles, so that he uses the target:
'Any?'

Activity 2:

Target:
Anything, anybody, anyone
(see activities for something, nothing).
Ask:
'(Is) anything/anybody/anyone (in the box)?'
Reply:
'Nobody/somebody/nothing.'

Activity 3:

Target:
Anybody/anyone.

Materials:
Picture lotto.
Share out the cards and loose pictures, leaving a selection of the pictures upside down on the table. Each 'player' must then ask:
'(Has) anybody/anyone got (the apple)?'
The appropriate picture must be given to him. If it is amongst those lying on the table, he misses his turn.

Every, everything, everybody, everyone

Activity:

Materials:
If you are not working with a group, use pictures of people or objects with similar and different attributes: several boys with the same coloured hair; boys with different coloured clothes; houses with the same number of windows or doors; household objects with a single attribute in common.
Studying a single series at a time ask:
'Does everyone have brown hair/a red shirt?'
'Does every (house) have three windows/one door?'
'Does everything have legs/a handle?'

Note: See Adjectives for **every**.

Both, few, many, each, several, most, least, much, next, first, last, second, etc.

Activity 1:

Target:
Both, few, many, several, most, least.

Materials:
Raisins, peanuts, blocks, marbles.
Take turns sharing out the objects, using the target utterances:
'(Do you want) a few/many?'
'You've got the most/least.'

Note:
Use only two objects to elicit **both**. Don't attempt to teach all these words at once – select one or two per session. Be sure the child has a turn to share out the objects and to comment appropriately.

Activity 2:

Target:
Each/both.

Materials:
Tokens, two model dolls.
Share out the tokens, using the target utterance:
One for each (person).
A ball for both.

> ## Activity 3:
> **Target:**
> Next, first, last, second etc.
> (**Note**: these items may also be used as adverbs:
>
>   He jumps first.
>   You go next.)
>
> As pronouns, remember they replace nouns or noun phrases:
> The next is Ken, last comes Peta.
>
> **Materials:**
> Model farm animals, a fence.
> Line up the animals and activate them to jump over the fence or instruct the child to do so:
> 'First is the pig.'
> 'Next is the cow.'
> 'Last is the dog.'

> **Variation:**
> If you are working with a group, create an obstacle course from classroom furniture, allowing each child to negotiate it while you instruct:
> 'First is Ralph. Next is Peta. Last is Gary.'
> Allow each child a turn to be 'teacher'.

Personal pronouns

Lee (1974) classifies reflexive and possessive pronouns as personal, whereas Quirk *et al*. (1972) categorises 'central' pronouns as:

Personal: I/me, we/us

Reflexive: myself, ourselves, oneself

Possessive: my/mine, our/ours

Personal pronouns avoid the repetition of a noun, and may serve to tie sentences together within a linguistic context (anaphora):
   The boy fell. He hurt his knee. His mother washed the knee and she put a bandage on it.

Personal Pronouns have the following characteristics:

1) *Subjective/object case:*

This refers to the position of the pronoun in the sentence:
> I go home (Subject).
> Mommy baths me (Object).

Subjective: I, we, he, she, they, who.
Objective: Me, us, him, her, them, who, whom.

2) *Person-distinction:*
1st person: The speaker – I, we.
2nd person: The person(s) addressed – you, etc.
3rd person: 'The rest', i.e., one or more persons or things mentioned - he/she/it/they etc.

3) *Gender contrast:*
The 3rd person singular of personal, reflexive, and possessive pronouns is distinguished by the masculine (he/him/himself/his), feminine (she/her/herself/hers) and neuter (it/itself/its) genders.

4) *Number:*
Distinction between singular and plural:
I/we, he/them.

Reflexive Pronouns

These end in -self (singular) and -selves (plural). These suffixes are added to determiner possessives (myself, ourselves) or objective case personal pronouns (himself, itself). Reflexive pronouns 'reflect' another element of the sentence, usually the subject:
> He fed himself.

Possessive pronouns

These consist of two groups:

The **attributive** (my, your etc.) which Quirk *et al.* (1972) classify as determiners, and the **predicative nominal** (mine, yours etc.). **Genitive** pronouns include: my, our, his, her, their, whose. (Quirk *et al.* 1972, Pink and Thomas 1970, Lund and Duchan 1983, Lee 1974.) Lee (1974) lists the problems in the pronoun usage of children:

> 1) *Failure to delete the noun or noun phrase which is replaced by the pronoun:*
> Mommy gave it the ball to me.
> 2) *Choice of incorrect pronoun:*
> The girl likes his own room.
> 3) *Plural forms develop late.*
> 4) *Case confusion:*
> She is visiting she's Granny.
> Due to the complexity of the English pronoun system, this grammatical form requires much remediation.

Relative pronouns

Relative pronouns introduce relative clauses and include: who, whom, whose, which, what and that. Lee (1974) includes: whichever, whatever and whoever. They are called 'relative' because they relate to a noun or pronoun, and may have two functions:

> 1) Acting as a pronoun in the subject, object or prepositional complement position.
> (See Book Two – Stage V: Subord S,C & O, and Postmodifiers.)
> 2) Acting as a prepositional complement when the preposition is end-placed and thus separated from the relative pronoun:
> This is the man whom you spoke to.
> The 'wh' word replaces the repeated item and the whole sentence modifies the first sentence. It acts as a pronoun rather than a conjunction because it is an integral part of the second sentence (clause).

Children usually first use 'wh' pronouns as modifiers of the object of a sentence because the word order doesn't change:

>That's the bike that I want.

It is more difficult to use the 'wh' pronoun to define the subject, as this requires the child to embed one sentence within another:

>The girl that I like is coming to play.

Some children confuse 'wh' pronouns in terms of their functions as questions or subordinates. The word order is then confused:

>I know what is that.
>
>He told me why was he crying.

(Lee 1974, Pink and Thomas 1970, Quirk *et al.* 1972.)

>**Note**: Lee also includes the adjective **how many** and **how much** under personal pronouns (see Adjectives).

Activities to teach personal pronouns

I, me, my, mine, you, your(s)

Activity 1:

Target:
I/you.
While the child is performing an action, ask:
'What are you doing?'
Assist him to respond:
'I'm jumping!'
Reverse roles, so that he describes your actions:
'You('re) sitting.'
Accept his probable omission of the auxilliary:
'I jumping.'
'You sitting.'
Keep modelling the correct form for him.

Activity 2:

Target:
I want, I do.

Materials:
A selection of toys.
Ask him:
'What do you want?'
Insist that he gives you the full sentence in reply:
I want the ...
(**Note**: this is not necessary in conversation, but our target for this exercise is the pronoun 'I'!)

Variation:
Ask him:
'Do you want the...?'
The response:
'I do/don't.'

Activity 3:

Target:
I('ve) got.
Take turns describing clothing:
'I('ve) got a (red jersey) – you('ve) got a (blue jersey).'

Activity 4:

Target:
You.
Take turns being teacher. (This is often more effective if you allot a special seat for the purpose and supply a pointer for a 'prop'.)
Teacher then instructs you or the group members to act:
'You – jump!'
'You – fall!'
(See Book Two – +s.)

Activity 5:

Target:
I/you take.

Materials:
Varied picture cards.
These may depict classes – fruit, furniture, vehicles.
Indicate that each 'player' must collect a single class of objects.
Place all the cards face upwards between you. Select the appropriate cards while describing your actions:
'I take the chair.'
'I take the table.'
'You take the car.'
'You take the bus.'
Allow the child to comment and instruct in this manner.

Activity 6:

Target:
You, me, mine, yours.

Materials:
Blocks, raisins, or tokens.
Share out the objects:
'(One block) for you/me.'
or:
'(This is) mine/yours.'

Variation:
Use personal possessions:
'(This is) my/your hat/bag.'

Activity 7:

Target:
Mine/yours (is)!

Materials:
Objects differing in a single characteristic: aeroplanes – red, yellow, blue; balls – big and small.
Each 'player' takes one plane and one ball and hides them behind his back. You ask:
'(Whose) plane (is) red?'
'Who(se) ball (is) big?'
The reply:
'Mine/yours (is).'

Activity 8:

Target:
I/you/my/your.

Materials:
Lotto.
Give each player a card, and share out the loose picture cards.
Take turns in selecting one card at a time:
'I('ve) got my/your...'
The 'winner' is the one who completes his card first.

Activity 9:

Target:
My/you and noun (a simple activity for a young child).

Materials:
Model animals – two of each. Share out all the animals:
'My lion, your lion, my dog, your dog.'
Allow the child to identify all the animals as you place them before each participant.

Activity 10:

Target:
My/your turn.

Materials:
Any toy to be activated, eg. Jack-in-the-box.
Keep asking:
'Whose turn?'
Insist that the child reply:
'Your turn/ my turn'
before you or he manipulate(s) it.

He, him, his, she, her, hers

Use all the activities described for teaching I, me, mine, you and your(s). Incorporate a third person by using a model doll, puppet or group member. Introduce a male or female first, but not both together. Confine the activity to a single case at first: he/she, or him/her.

Finally introduce both sexes and vary the case:

> He wants his...; She wants her...

Use sequence stories to reinforce the correct use of the personal pronouns.

Activity 1:

Target:
He/his – he wants his...; or she/her – she wants her...

Materials:
Cut-out dolls and clothing; the Peabody Kit
(see Book One, Equipment).
Introduce the doll(s):
'This is a boy/girl. He/she('s) cold.'
'He/she wants his/her pants/shirt/shoes.'
Allow the child to select the appropriate items and doll. Reverse roles, allowing him to use the target utterance.

167

Activity 2:

Target:
Him/her.
For him/her.

Materials:
As in Activity 1. Select items of clothing and appropriately dress the dolls: for him/her.

Activity 3:

Target:
He/she scratches/pulls/kisses him/her.

Materials:
Two male and two female dolls or puppets.
Activate the dolls appropriately or instruct one another to do so:
'He scratches her.'
'He pulls him.'

We, us, our(s), they, them, their

Use all the appropriate activities described above, substituting the plural form. If you are working with a single child, sit beside him and place the doll family opposite you so as to create two units:
'We want a ...'
'They want a ...'

These, those

See Indefinite Pronouns – **this**, **that**.

Reflexives: myself, yourself, himself, herself, itself, themselves

It is important that the child realises that this structure emphasises the subject.

Activity 1:

Target:
Myself/yourself.
Say:
'Come and jump with me.'
'We jump together.'
'Now, you jump by yourself.'
'I jump by myself.'
Allow the child to describe the varied interactions.

Activity 2:

Target:
Myself/yourself.

Materials:
A task to complete – undoing a zip or button, tying a bow. Assist the child to perform the task then allow him to complete it unaided. Use the appropriate targets and encourage him to do so too:
'I help you.'
'Do it yourself.'
'I do it (by) myself.'

Activity 3:

Target:
Himself/herself.

Materials:
Pictures of people performing tasks, model dolls.
Use activities 1 and 2, substituting a third person in the form of a group member or doll. Alternatively, describe the pictures appropriately:
'He dresses himself.'

Note: It is useful to contrast pictures as follows:
'Mommy dressing a boy/girl.'
'The girl/boy dressing him/herself.'
'Mommy feeding a child.'
'The child feeding him/herself.'

Activity 4:

Target:
Itself.

Materials:
Model animals.
Use all the appropriate activities described above:
'Is the pig running with the dog?'
'No, it's running by itself.'
'The girl is scratching the dog.'
'The dog is scratching itself.'

Activity 5:

Target:
Themselves.
Use all the appropriate activities described above, substituting the plural form:
'They are scratching themselves.'

Note: Children often substitute the incorrect case: they-selves. This requires constant modelling.

Wh-pronouns

Who, which, whose, whom, what, that, how many, how much

Note: For all references to Co-ordinating, Subordinating or Post-modifying Clauses and Phrases, see LARSP V – Book Two. The activities which follow utilise the subordinate clause mainly in the objectival position, as do most young children when learning language (Crystal 1982).

Who/whose/whom

Activity 1:

Target:
This is the man who rides a bike.
This is the boy who's washing his dog.
A man who is digging in the garden.
A girl who's holding an ice cream.

Materials:
Picture cards or models depicting attributes as in the above-mentioned examples. Describe each picture or model appropriately, choosing the structure most appropriate for the child:
'This is the man who is digging in the garden.'
'The girl who is digging in the garden.'
Turn the cards upside down, or hide the models about the room. Take turns in guessing the identity before turning up the picture or revealing the model.

Variation:

Target:
This is the lady whom I like.

Materials:
Pictures of models. Take turns selecting the model of your choice while using the target utterance.

Note: This is not a form used by most children. In formal English, **whom** is used when the preposition appears before the relative pronoun, as in: The boy to whom I gave a message.

However, the preposition is usually moved to the end of the clause, and **whom** is either omitted or replaced by **that**:
The girl that I gave the doll to.

In the object position, it is replaced by **who** or **that**:
The girl who I saw.
The girl that I saw. (Pink and Thomas 1970)

Activity 2:

Target:
This/that/those is/are who I like/want.

Materials:
Pictures of models as in the activity described above. Note the omission of the complement, lady, thus changing the form:
This is (the lady) who I like.

Which

Activity 1:

Target:
The boy/girl is eating an apple/banana which is red/green/yellow.

Materials:
Picture cards representing:
A boy eating a red apple
A boy eating a green apple
A boy eating a yellow banana
A boy eating a green banana
A girl eating a red apple
A girl eating a green apple, etc.

Having described each picture appropriately, turn them face downwards. Take turns guessing the correct subject matter before revealing each picture. If the target is too difficult for the child, omit the subject and verb: A banana which is yellow.

This work can be combined with activities to teach questions, as these are interrogative pronouns.

Activity 2:

Target:
(Give me) the animal which has stripes.

Materials:
Model animals.
Take turns in describing the animals:
'(Give me) the animal which has a long trunk.'

Activity 3:

Target:
You know which is mine.

Materials:
Coloured models: red and blue planes; red and blue balls; red and blue tokens.
Give the child a token, indicating that his colour is red and yours is blue. Now, assist him to hold up both planes. Say:
'You know which is mine!'
When he has shared out the models appropriately, reverse roles, indicate that you've forgotten which player has the red objects and which has the blue. Assist him to use the target utterance.

What

Activity 1:

Target:
Do/don't do what I do!
Carry out a series of actions – clapping hands, raising your arms, jumping, etc. After each one say:
'Do/don't do what I do.'
The child must obey your commands. Reverse roles so that he issues the commands.

Activity 2:

Target:
I can see what you drew.

Materials:
Tracing paper.
Allow the child to draw a picture. He holds it up to the light. You say:
'I can see what you drew – a horse!'
Reverse roles and assist him to use the target utterance.

Activity 3:

Target:
I'll/I won't take/eat what you take/eat.

Materials:
Foodstuffs or toys – two of each object. Allow the child to select an item.
Say:
'I'll take/eat or I won't take/eat what you take/eat',
and act appropriately. Reverse roles so that you make the first selection and the child uses the appropriate utterance.

Activity 4:

Target:
I know what you've got.

Materials:
Three objects – a ball, a car, a boat.
Assist the child to conceal each one one at a time in his hand. You say:
'I know what you've got – the boat.'
When you've guessed all three correctly, reverse roles.

That

Young children as well as adults tend to replace who, which, whose and whom with that. All the activities described for use with these wh pronouns may therefore be utilised when teaching that. Here are a few more examples:

Activity 1:

Target:
Post-modifying Clause.

Materials:
Model animals or picture cards.
Ask the child to give you:
'The animal (one) that barks/hops/can fly.'

Variation:

Use fruit: The (one) that is juicy/red/sour.
Reverse roles so that the child uses the target utterance.

Activity 2:

Materials:
A variety of objects with obvious attributes – a round/flat/square shape; a dirty/clean object; something to eat/drink etc.
Hiding one object at a time say:
'(I have) something that is round/flat/dirty/we can drink.'
Once again reverse roles so that the child uses the target utterance.

How many/how much

Activity:

Target:
(Tell me) how many you want.
(Tell me) how much it costs.

Materials:
Money, and other 'props' to create a 'shopping' activity.
Role play with the child using the target utterances:
'Tell me/show me how many eggs.'
'Tell me how much sugar.'
'Tell me how much money.'

Variation:

Play school. Teach one another simple maths using props if necessary:
'Tell me (show me) how many apples are here.'

(His) own, one, oneself, whichever, whoever, whatever

One/oneself

Target:
One can easily lose oneself.
No activities are offered to teach this structure, as young children are unlikely to use these forms in context. They are more likely to use the more colloquial form:
You can easily get lost.

Own

> **Activity:**
>
> **Target:**
> I must use my own.
>
> **Materials:**
> Possessions such as clothing, pencils, school cases, school lunch. Acting out the use of each item say:
> 'This isn't my pencil/lunch/case/jersey. It's yours. I mustn't use yours. I must use my own.'
> Encourage the child to use this structure in appropriate contexts.

Whichever/whoever/whatever

The significant semantic feature in these forms lies in the aspect of choice.

> **Activities:**
>
> **Target:**
> You can eat whatever you like.
> I'll choose whichever one wins the race.
> The prize is for whoever builds the highest block tower.
> Build a block bridge. Choose whoever you wish to help you. At this stage of language development these structures are best modelled appropriately in context, and may be emphasised when you are narrating a story.

3. Verbs

The verb (V) is an action or doing word, and it is the most important element in the clause because it governs other patterns in the rest of the sentence (Crystal *et al.* 1976). In a clause the verb has a subject (S):
The boy (S) sings (V),
unless the V is used as a command:

> Go!

Some verbs govern an object (O) where the action is performed directly upon that O: He (S) washed (V) the dishes (O).

There may also be an indirect O added to this: He (S) gave (V) the cup (O_d) to her (O_i).

Intransitive verbs do not perform an action on an object:

> He (S) came (V) to my house (Adverbial A).

Some verbs govern a complement (C) which is an element specifying something more about the S or O: He (S) is (V) cross (C).

When the verb to be appears in isolation thus, it is known as the **copula**. It is the main verb, and undergoes the same tense, number and person elaboration as the auxiliary (aux) does.

Verb phrases consist either of a main verb or of one or more auxiliary verbs and a main verb, for example:

> I have been reading.

There are two types of **auxiliaries**: primary auxiliary verbs and modal auxiliary verbs.

Main Verbs		Write, jump, frighten, eat
Auxiliary Verbs	*Primary*	do, have, be
	Modal	can, may, shall, will, could might, should, would, used to must, ought to, need, dare

Table 5: Types of verbs - main and auxiliary. (Adapted from *A Grammar Of Contemporary English*, by R. Quirk, S. Greenbaum, J. Leech and J. Swartvik, Longman Group UK 1972, p. 69.)

There are two kinds of verb phrase: finite and non-finite. **Finite verbs** contain the verb as their first and only word, and it is the finite verb which carries tense, for example:

> He walked.

The **non-finite** forms of the verb are the infinitive, the -ing participle and the -ed participle. These are what Lee (1974) calls 'secondary verbs'. In Book Two we learnt about therapy with components of the verb, particularly the main verbs and auxiliaries. But the development of the non-finite verb phrases tends to be a later developing aspect which occurs in complex sentences. Lee provides the detailed description and developmental sequence of the non-finite verb, which is not fully considered on the LARSP by the category VP (LARSP Stages V and VI).

The development of the verb system in English is a complicated matter as we have seen, and it influences the acquisition of a number of grammatical forms, such as questions and negatives.

Verbs may take many different forms to differentiate meaning, which they do by varying inflections:

> Jump/jumped/jumping,

and by varying word form:

> Eat/ate.

Verb forms may vary according to:

1) Person and number:
Verbs agree with a subject
1st person singular: I sit.
3rd person singular: He sits.

2) Voice:
A verb is in the active voice when the person or thing denoted by the subject performs the action:
He jumps.
The passive voice is demonstrated when a person or thing denoted by the subject suffers an action:
The bike was ridden by him.

3) Tense and aspect:
(a) The continuance of action:
I am sitting
I was sitting
I shall be sitting
I should be sitting

(b) Time of action:
Present, past, future or future in the past:
I go
I went
I will go
I would go

Simple past tenses are marked by verb inflection:
Played
or by irregular verbs:
Ran/run
(See Irregular Past Verbs, below).
The future is marked by the auxiliary:
Will run

(Crystal *et al*.1976, Courtman Davies 1979, Pink and Thomas 1970, Quirk *et al*. 1972.)

(c) The completeness of an action:
I have seen
I had seen
I shall have seen
I should have seen

Tense is thus particularly variable according to the meaning or the use of the verb. For example simple past tense:

>The boy walked,

describes an event which took place in the past at a given time or period. The progressive tense, however, indicates that the action is temporary – it is an 'action in progress instead of the occurrence of action or the existence of a state':

>The boy was walking.

(Quirk *et al*. 1972, p.93)

Note the variety of inflections and auxiliaries used to form verb tenses, seen in Table 6.

Present	Simple Continuous Perfect Perfect Continuous	He works He is working He has worked He has been working
Past	Simple Continuous Perfect Perfect Continuous	He worked He was working He had worked He had been working
Future	Simple Continuous Perfect Perfect Continuous	He will work He will be working He will have worked He will have been working
Present Perfect	Conditional Continuous Conditional Conditional Continuous	He would work He would be working He would have worked He would have been working

Table 6: Statements denoting verb tenses – active voice

These verb forms correspond to the main and secondary verbs in the developmental sentence scoring chart (Lee 1974).

Uninflected verbs

These verbs do not vary their form to indicate person, number, voice or tense:
>Jump, sit, fall, run.

Copula is or 's:

It's red, it is big (LARSP Stage III, Word).
Other forms include:
>Am, are, was, were.

In sentences where there is a co-referential relation between the subject and the subject complement, the verb acts as a link and has little meaning in itself. It can be dispensed with:
>The man who is tall – the tall man.

The verb to be is described as the 'typical, colourless copula' (Quirk *et al.* 1972, p.820). Other copulas which have more intrinsic meaning than **be** include:

> appear: I appear happy.
> become: They become naughtier.

Young children do not usually use these forms.

Auxiliary verbs

Auxiliary verbs include the primary auxiliaries **do**, **have** and **be**, and the modal auxiliaries.

Do

Do may be used for support (obligatory do). It carries little meaning in itself but is required to form tense, the negative or the question, and to complete the sentence grammatically (Lee 1974).

> Don't you want to come?

Emphatic do

Do may receive stress in a sentence such as:

> Marilyn **did** say she'd be late, didn't she?
> Andrea, **do** stop wriggling!

Auxiliaries appear in different forms to indicate present and past tense;

> Have/had, is/were, do/did,

and according to the person of the subject:

> I have, he has, I am, she is, you do, he does.

They also take elided forms:

> I've/you've.

This is often confusing for those learning English as a second language.

We have therefore attempted to reflect the structural variation of the auxiliaries most commonly used in South African English, below. Note that the modal auxiliaries do not vary according to person, as do the primary auxiliaries (Janks 1989). Quirk *et al.* (1972) use clear and comprehensive tables to record the various forms of the auxiliary. We refer our readers to their tables for a more comprehensive description of the English auxiliary.

Forms of auxiliary verbs commonly used

The auxiliary be

This verb has two functions:

1) To indicate the progressive tense:
>He is falling.
>He was falling.

2) To indicate the passive:
>The bike was ridden by the boy
>(see Passive voice and LARSP V).

Progressive tense

Present tense

1st Person singular
Positive: I am coming/ I'm coming.
Negative: I am not coming/ I'm not coming.
Question: Am I coming/ Aren't I coming/ Am I not coming?

2nd person singular and plural
Positive: You are coming/ You're coming.
Negative: You are not coming/ You're not coming/ You aren't coming.
Question: Are you coming/ Aren't you coming/ Are you not coming?

3rd person singular
Positive: He/she/it is coming/ He/she/it's coming.
Negative: He/she/it is not coming/ He/she/it's not coming/ He/she/it isn't coming.
Question: Is he/she/it coming/ Isn't he/she/it coming/ Is he/she/it not coming?

1st and 3rd person plural
Positive: We/They are coming/ We/they're coming.
Negative: We/they are not coming/ We/they're not coming/ We aren't coming.
Question: Are we/they coming/ Are we/they not coming/ Aren't we/they coming?

Past tense

1st and 3rd person singular
Positive: I /he/she/it was coming.
Negative: I he/she/it was not coming/ I/he/she/it wasn't coming.
Question: Was I/he/she/it coming/ Wasn't I/he/she/it coming/ Was I/he/she/it not coming?

2nd person singular and plural, and 1st and 3rd person plural
Positive: You/we/they were coming.
Negative: You/we/they were not coming/ You/we/they weren't coming.
Question: Were you/we/they coming/ Weren't you/we/they coming/ Were you/we/they not coming?

Note: The main verb **come** in the examples cited above takes the -ing form.
Be may also appear in the -ed participle form as in:
He had been crying.

The auxiliary have

Have as an auxiliary combines with past participles to form perfective complex verb phrases (Quirk *et al* 1972).

Positive forms:

I have been to town/ I've been to town.
He/she has been to town/ He/she's been to town.
He/she had been to town/ He'd/she'd been to town.
Having been to town...

Negative forms:

I have not been to town/ I've not been to town/ I haven't been to town.
She has not been to town/ She's not been to town/ She hasn't been to town.
They had not been to town/ They'd not been to town/ They hadn't been to town.
Not having been to town, he didn't buy his hat.

Question forms:

Have you been to town/ Haven't you been to town?
Has he been to town/ Hasn't he been to town?
Had he been to town/ Hadn't he been to town?

The modal auxiliaries

Certainty (logical probability)

The following modal auxiliaries are more commonly used in South Africa:

Can (ability or permission)
Positive: I can go.
Negative: I cannot go/ I can not go/ I can't go.
Question: Can you go/ Can't you go/ Can I not go?

Could
Positive: I could go.
Negative: I could not go/ I couldn't go.
Question: Could I go/ Couldn't I go?

May
Positive: I may go.
Negative: I may not go.
Question: May I go?

Should (Obligation)
Positive: I should go.
Negative: I should not go/ I shouldn't go.
Question: Should I go/ Shouldn't I go/ Should I not go?

Will
Positive: I will go.
Negative: I will not go/ I won't go.
Question: Will I go/ Won't I go/ Will I not go?

'll
Positive: I'll go.
(Negative form seldom used.)

'd
Positive: I'd go.
(Negative form seldom used.)

Would
Positive: I would go.
Negative: I would not go/ I wouldn't go.
Question: Would I go/ Wouldn't I go?

Must
Positive: I must go.
Negative: I must not go/ I mustn't go.
Question: Must I go/ Mustn't I go?

Ought to
Positive: I ought to go.
(Negative and question forms seldom used.)

Used to
Positive: I used to go.
(Negative and question forms seldom used.)

Emphatic

3rd Person singular
Positive: He/she/it does go.
Negative: He/she/it does not go/ doesn't go.
Question: Does he/she/it go/ Doesn't he/she/it go?

3rd Person Plural
Positive: They do go.
Negative: They don't go.
Question: Do they go?

Past tense forms

Positive: He did go.
Negative: I did not go/didn't go.
Question: Did/didn't you go?

Tags (LARSP Stage IV)

Daniel waits. Doesn't he?
Daniel doesn't wait, does he?
Daniel waited, didn't he?
Daniel didn't wait, did he?

These verbs aid other verbs to vary in time, tense and aspect. They may be used with infinitives to indicate possibility, permission, ability, obligation, etc. Auxiliary verbs are particularly important for certain constructions, such as negatives and questions. Thus they are crucial for the child's development of language.

The passive voice

(See LARSP Stage VI.)

Pink and Thomas (1970, pp.36-37) state that 'Voice is that form of the verb which shows whether the person or thing denoted by the subject acts, or is acted upon... A verb is said to be in the Passive Voice when the person or thing denoted by the subject undergoes or suffers an action.'

> Active Voice: Mpho chopped down the tree.
> Passive Voice: The tree was chopped down by Mpho.

Only transitive verbs that take an object can be turned into the passive. The passive voice is used when it is more convenient or interesting to stress the thing that is being done than the person or thing doing the action, and when the doer is not known.

The passive tense is formed by putting the verb **be** into the same tense as the active verb and adding the past participle of the active verb:

> The window has been broken by Gary.

The verb **get** may also be used in the passive, but it is usually confined to sentences without an expressed subject:

> The window got broken. (Quirk *et al.* 1972)

When the agent or doer of the action is mentioned in the passive voice, it is preceded by **by**:

> Active Voice: John rode the bike.
> Passive Voice: The bike was ridden by John.

However, in the case of materials the preposition used is **with**:

> Active Voice: The water filled the glass.
> Passive Voice: The glass was filled with water.

Lee (1974) lists only the following passives on the Developmental Sentence Chart:

Main verbs: passive with **get**, any tense
              passive with **be**, any tense.

Secondary verbs: passive infinitival complement:
With get:
I have to get dressed.
I don't want to get hurt.
With be:
I want to be pulled.
It's going to be locked.

Lee cautions that it is difficult to know whether children have really mastered the passive sentence rules, or whether they are merely 'repeating certain over-used, stereotyped forms' (Lee 1974, pp 35-36).

Crystal *et al* (1976) anticipate the appearance of the passive between ages three and a half to four and a half, as recorded on the LARSP (Stage VI).

Non-finite verb phrases

These are referred to by Lee (1974) as secondary verbs, and occur in complex sentences, hence involving analysis at Stages V and VI on the LARSP. Lee defines secondary verbs as infinitives, participles and gerunds (which occur in complex sentences). The non-finite clause has the ability to do without a subject and has no distinctions of person or number, nor does it have any modal auxiliaries.

Infinitive complement

This form is appropriate on some occasions when one basic sentence is the object of another basic sentence. If the subjects of the two sentences are the same, the subject of the infinitive is omitted:

>Lerato wanted to go.

But when the subjects of the two sentences are different, the second subject is stated in the objective case:

>Lerato wants you to go.

With some verbs the infinitive **to** is omitted:

>I heard the bugle (to) blow.

These verbs include:

>Can, do, dare, may, must, need, shall, will.

Infinitives may also be used as second objects after **like**, **feel**, **hear**, **see**, **make** (Quirk *et al.* 1972).

Non-complementing infinitives

These are not as common as complementing infinitives, for example: Made him go.

a) Infinitives as subjects

In conversational speech these are seldom used:

>To run in the rain is fun.

b) Infinitives showing purpose or reason:

>Peta went there to fetch her book.

The subject of the infinitive may be omitted if it is the same as the main sentence:

>He stopped to talk.

c) Wh-word + infinitive:

>I know where to look.
>I know what to do.

Children's development of the infinitive

Lee (1974, p.50-52) states that children begin to use 'primitive' infinitival forms early. These are contracted and may be stereotyped forms or 'giant words' rather than rule governed syntactic features.
She lists these as follows:

> ### *Five early-developing infinitives*
> I 'wanna' see (want to see).
> I'm 'gonna' see (going to see).
> I 'gotta' see (have got to see).
> 'Lemme' (to) see (let me (to) see).
> Let's (to) play (let (us to) play) (LARSP III, let XY).

It is important to note that these are common in American English, but not all of these forms are used by all English speakers. However, the form 'let XY' is marked on the LARSP.

Lee cannot stipulate the order in which other uses of the infinitive appear, but states that the subjectival infinitive is never heard in children's speech.

Some children delete the entire infinitive if its meaning is clear in context:

> I know what.
> I know how.
>
> Other children include the infinitive marker **to**, but not the lexical verb: I know how to.

Clinically, children often omit the infinitive marker **to**:

> I want come.

Alternatively they manage to include **to**, but exclude the auxiliary or lexical verb:

> The boy gonna find it.

Gerunds and participles

In joining sentences together, the verb of the second sentence may appear as an adjective or noun within the first sentence.

Gerunds

When a verb is used as a noun it is called a gerund. Gerunds carry the suffix **–ing** and may be used as follows:

>*As subject*: Dancing is very enjoyable.
>*As object*: I love dancing.
>*Complement*: My favourite recreation is dancing.
>*Gerund governed by a preposition*: I keep fit by dancing.

Participles

The participle acts like a verb in a second sentence but appears in adjectival form:

>*Before a noun*: He turned off the running tap.
>*Predicatively*: Mommy went out shopping.
>I heard the boy crying in the playground.
>
>*Introducing an adjective phrase*:
>Opening the bottle, he took a long drink of milk.
>The participle may be in the past tense:
>She has a grandson named Daniel.

We recognise participles used with auxiliaries in the compound verb forms to form continuous tenses and the passive voice:

>The window is breaking;
>The window was breaking;
>The window was broken.

Children's verb development

Verb forms, as can be seen, are complicated in English, and language-disabled children have a great deal of difficulty in mastering them, although according to Whetnell (cited by Courtman-Davies, 1979), a normal three-year-old uses approximately 200 verbs.

Most children begin with the uninflected verb – jump, fall (Lee 1976, Crystal 1974) – and only thereafter do they begin to use such verb forms as **is** and **-ing**:

>Is eating.

This is very important to note, as many language programmes introduce the present continuous form **is** + **ing** first, which is contrary to normal child language development. This verb form is particularly difficult for the hearing-impaired child, as is the copula **is**. It is difficult to hear or to lip-read, and is frequently omitted:

>Daddy walking.
>The dog big.

(Manually coding the auxiliaries helps to remind the hearing-impaired child of its presence, and Lee suggests teaching it in interrogative form first).

As we have noted in Book Two, irregular verbs – for example **go**, **went** – develop in the correct past tense form, and are sometimes changed to conform to the child's notion of regular past tense (go, goed) at a later stage, thus illustrating rule-governed learning (Slobin, cited by Lee 1974; Menyuk 1971).

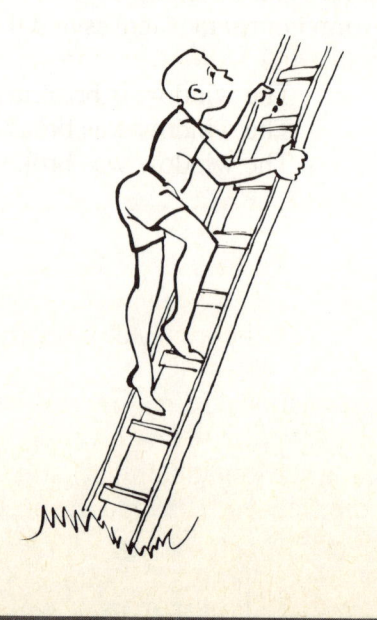

Irregular past tense verbs which may be used by children

(From the complete list of irregular verbs in *A Grammar Of Contemporary English*, by R. Quirk, S. Greenbaum, G. Leech and J. Swartvik, Longman Group UK 1972, pp. 119–121.)

*be (see auxiliaries is/are/was/were); beat – beat – beaten; begin – began – begun; bend – bent; *bite – bit – bitten; bleed – bled; *blow – blew – blown; *break – broke – broken; *bring – brought; *build – built; burn – burnt; burst – burst; *buy – bought; can – (see auxiliary can/could); *catch – caught; choose – chose – chosen; *come – came ; *cut – cut; *dig – dug; *do – (see auxiliary do/did); *draw – drew; dream – dreamt; *drink – drank; *drive – drove – driven; *eat – ate – eaten; *fall – fell – fallen; *feed – fed; feel – felt; *fight – fought; * find – found; *fly – flew; forget – forgot – forgotten; freeze – froze; *get – got; *give – gave – given; go – went; *grow – grew – grown; hang – hung; *have – had; hear – heard; * hide – hid – hidden; hit – hit;* hold – held; *hurt – hurt; keep – kept; kneel – knelt; knit – knit; *know – knew – known; learn – learnt; leave – left; lend – lent; *let – let; *lie – lay; light – lit; *lose – lost; *make – made; may – (see auxiliary may/might); meet – met; *put – put;*read – read; *ride – rode – ridden; *run – ran; say – said; *see – saw – seen; sell – sold; sent – sent; shake – shook – shaken; shine – shone; shoot – shot; *shut – shut; *sing – sang (sung); sink – sank – sunk; sit – sat; *sleep – slept; *slide – slid; smell – smelt; speak – spoke; spell – spelt; spend – spent; spill – spilt; spin – spun; *stand – stood; steal – stole; *stick – stuck; *sting – stung; swear – swore – sworn; sweep – swept; *swim – swam – swum; *take – took – taken; teach – taught; *tear – torn; tell – told; think – thought; *throw – threw – thrown; understand – understood; *wake – woke – woken; wear – wore; *wet – wet; will – (see auxiliary will/would); win – won; wind – wound; *write – wrote – written.

Note:
We have marked with an asterisk all those verbs which we believe may be more frequently used by the younger child.

Certain modal forms emerge first in their negative form: can't, won't. They are treated by the child as a single word. Some modals appear first in the past tense (should, might), as children are exposed to these in adult speech more frequently than to the present tense forms (shall, may) (Lee 1974).

The development of early infinitives is discussed in this chapter under the heading Secondary Verbs. Participles may develop earlier than gerunds, as they are more frequently in use:

>That's a man washing his car.

Gerunds often first appear in a stereotyped, almost idiomatic form:

>He started crying.
>We went riding.

and are used very early in the child's language development in this form (LARSP III, SVO).

Only in advanced teaching of language, according to Lee, would a clinician introduce gerunds at all, that is, at Stage V LARSP. She suggests they could be taught as a substitute for infinitives:

I like to cook - I like cooking (Lee 1974).

Activities to teach the verb

Young children should be encouraged to act out the verbs they learn.

Uninflected verbs: jump, sit, fall, run

First verbs should be selected according to their frequency of occurrence in daily activities, and should describe definite actions (Courtman-Davies 1979). They should also be fun to do. Let the child act on command:

>'Jump! run!'

and give the same instruction to puppets and dolls. Uninflected verbs are easily used in isolation in this form. Pictures or stick-figure drawings may supplement action at first, but will be used with the older child to illustrate verbs not easily enacted.

When resorting to pictures, try to depict the verb in varying contexts. The verb charts published by Dormac Co. present eight pictures for each verb:

>blow – the wind is blowing, the windmill is blowing, the girl blows out her candles, the boy is blowing bubbles, etc.

Copula is or 's

Activity 1:

Materials:
Objects known to the child.
Display one object at a time and say:
'This is a (car).'
Reverse roles, so the child uses the target utterance.

Note :
This is an excellent activity for teaching the negative. As you display each article, misname it,
'This is a car!' (showing him the shoe).
He will enjoy correcting you.
'No, it's not. It's a shoe!'

Activity 2:

Target:
Is that a ball? No, it's not!

Materials:
6 common objects, or a variety of coloured tokens.
Show the objects to the child and describe them:
'This is a ball.'
'This is a yellow block.'
Assist the child to hide one in his fist. Guess:
'Is that a ball/yellow block?'
Model the answer if he is unable to reply:
'Yes/no it's not/it is!'
Reverse roles and assist him to guess the contents of your hand, using the target utterance.

Activity 3:

Target:
Is the clown happy? No, he's not/ no, he isn't/ yes, he is!

Materials:
Pictures depicting opposites: a big boy/a small boy, a dirty shoe/ a clean shoe, a happy clown/a sad clown.
Describe each picture, then place them face downwards in matching pairs. Take turns in selecting a picture, but do not show it to one another. The other 'player' then guesses:
'Is the clown (happy)?'
The reply:
'No, he's not/yes, he is!'

Variation:
(for children at stage V on the LARSP – see Book Two.)

Target:
Is the clown happy or is he sad?
Encourage the child to use this compound utterance when guessing what picture appears on the card.
(See Interrogative Reversals).

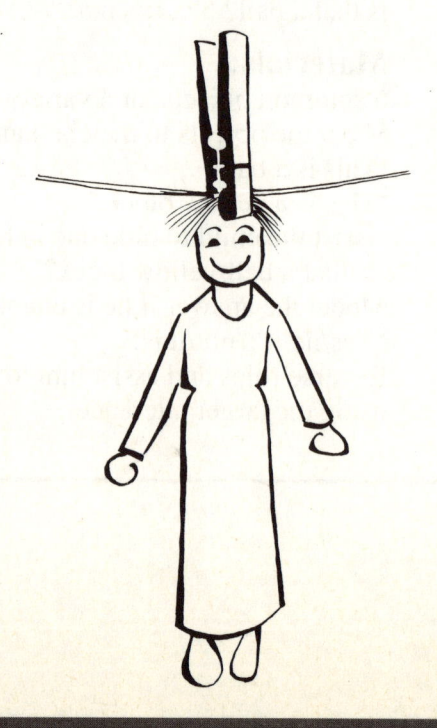

Is + verb + -ing: He is coming

Activity:

Target:
Is the boy (jumping)? No, he isn't/yes, he is (jumping).

Materials:
A model doll and furniture – a bed, a chair, a bath.
Assist the child to activate the doll behind a screen, indicating that you cannot see the action. The doll must sleep in the bed or sit on the chair, or take a bath. Then ask:
'Is (the boy) bathing?'
The response:
'No, he isn't!'
Keep guessing until you are correct, then reverse roles and allow the child to guess what the doll is doing.

Variation:
Use picture cards of a single subject acting: a boy jumping, a boy running, a boy hopping.
After describing each picture to the child, turn them face downwards. Take turns guessing which card is which before turning it over:
'This boy is running! He is/isn't/is not.'
You may use the question form by taking turns to hold a card, not revealing the picture to one another. The 'opponent' then guesses:
'Is the boy running?'

Note:
It is often advisable to teach the **ing** form before inserting the auxiliary **is**. Use the appropriate activities described above, asking the question:
'What is (the boy) doing?
'The child replies:
'Jumping! sleeping!'
(See Interrogative Reversals.)

-s and -ed: He plays, he played

(See also Book Two – LARSP, Word.)

Activity 1:
Ask the child questions:
'Where does a fish live?'
Reply:
'The fish lives in water.'
'What does a boy wear?'
'He wears a shirt.'

Note:
Encourage the child to reply in a full sentence here in order to use the target utterance. In conversational context the reply to your question, 'What does a boy wear?' would simply be, 'A shirt!'

Activity 2:

Target:
One zebra jumps – two zebras jump.

Materials:
Model animals or picture cards depicting: one zebra jumping, two zebras jumping; one elephant eating, two elephants eating; one monkey climbing, two monkeys climbing.
Placing the cards face downwards, encourage the child to describe the pictures appropriately as he reveals them. He may activate the models while he says:
'One zebra jumps, two elephants eat.'

Note:
This is a very difficult structure for the hearing-impaired child to learn. It carries no meaning and is not easy to hear or read on the lips. The use of a manual code and the written form is of some assistance.

-ed: regular past tense

Teach the past tense in contrast to the present tense. It is most important that the child understands the meaning of an action that is completed. Teaching the written form alone will not ensure this.

Activity 1:

Target:
Regular verbs – jump/jumped, hop/hopped, walk/walked, cry/cried.
Give the child a command:
'Jump!'
While he is jumping, command him to stop. Say:
'You've stopped (jumping). What did you do?'
Model the target:
'You jumped.'
Use a variety of verbs in this manner until he comprehends that the morphological marker **-ed** implies that the action has been completed.

Activity 2:

Target:
The girl will paint the house.
The girl is painting the house.
The girl painted the house.

Materials:
The Wilson Syntax Programme (see chapter on Equipment – Book One). You may make your own picture cards depicting a subject about to carry out an action; the subject in the process of doing so; and the subject after completing an action.

Place these pictures in sequence before the child. Describe one at a time while he indicates which picture is relevant to your description. Allow him to describe each picture appropriately himself.

Note:
You may omit the picture depicting future tense at this stage. Some easy verbs to illustrate include: bathing, eating, wiping, pushing.

Irregular past tense: ate, saw

Teach these as you taught the regular past **-ed**, but in the case of irregular verbs, every verb form must be used in context. To make these verbs meaningful and the task more motivating, introduce them in themes.

Activity 1:

Target:
Slept, woke, ate, drank, sat, read, drove.

Materials:
A doll's house, model dolls and furniture.
Manipulate the dolls through a series of related actions. Ask the child to describe these when you've completed the activity:
'Daddy slept. Then he woke up. He ate his breakfast. He drank his tea. He sat on a chair and read his paper. Then he drove to work.'

Activity 2:

Target:
Went, swam, built, burnt, rode.

Materials:
Sequence pictures depicting a child at the seaside.
Assist the child to describe the sequence of events:
'The boy went to the beach. He swam. He built a sandcastle. He bought an ice-cream He rode on a donkey. The sun burnt his back.'

Note:
Be sure not to use a single picture as this would call for a description using the present continuous tense: A boy is swimming in the sea. A girl is buying an ice-cream.

201

Copula: am, are, was, were

Activity 1:

Target:
Are.

Materials:
As for **is** (activity), but make sure that each picture card depicts at least two individuals with the same characteristic – two clowns laughing, two clowns who are sad etc.

Activity 2:

Target:
Am.

Materials:
One object to be hidden.
The child hides the object, and you ask continually as you hunt for it:
'Am I near (the ball)?'
Reverse roles so that he uses the target utterance.

Activity 3:

Target:
Are/am.

Materials:
Model animals.
Close your eyes and allow the child to place an animal in your hand. Feel it and guess:
'Are you an (elephant)?'
Encourage the child to reply on the animal's behalf:
'I am/I'm not.'
Reverse roles so that the child uses both target utterances.

Activity 4:

Target:
You are/you're.

Materials:
Provide cardboard cut-outs of animal characteristics: a trunk, a lion's mane, donkey ears etc.
Take turns selecting a cut-out and 'wearing' it while both players use the appropriate target utterance:
'You're an (elephant). No, I'm a donkey.'

Activity 5:

Target:
I am.

Materials:
None. (This activity is appropriate for a group).
Ask the children questions:
'Who is the biggest/smallest?'
The reply:
'I am!'

Activity 6:

Target:
Was/were.

Materials:
Water or sand, containers.
Remember that these copula forms represent past tense so be sure to use them appropriately. While the child is pouring the water or sand in and out of the containers, describe and discuss:
'The jug is full.'
'It was empty!'

Note:
Use two or more identical containers to elicit **were**.
'The cups were empty – now they are full.'

Activity 7:

Target:
Was/were.

Materials:
A toy garage and model cars.
Drive the car(s) in and out of the garage:
'The car(s) was/were in/out (of the garage).'
Use the question form (see Interrogative Reversals) by taking turns to place the car(s) in the garage or to hide them elsewhere. The other 'player' then looks in the garage. You ask him:
'Was/were the car(s) in (the garage)?'
Reply:
'No/yes, the car(s) was/were/wasn't/weren't in (the garage).'

Auxiliaries: am, are, was, were

Activity 1:

Target:
Am/are.

Materials:
None.
Encourage the child to act while you close your eyes:
'Are you jumping/sitting?'
Reply:
'I'm not jumping/I am!'
Remember to use the contracted form **I'm** where appropriate. Reverse roles, but if you need to model the target utterance for him, place his hand on his own chest so that he does not confuse roles (see also the Negative).

Activity 2:

Target:
Are.

Materials:
A variety of toys and models – a toy tea set, blocks, cars, etc.
Parallel play while you and the child use the target utterance:
'We're/we are pushing the cars/ having tea.'

Activity 3:

Target:
Are
(See **is + verb + -ing**, and Interrogative Reversals).

Note:
Be sure to have more than one subject, and to activate them together:
'Are the boys sleeping?'
When using picture cards, be sure that they depict more than a single subject, so that the plural auxiliary is appropriately used.

Variation:

Target:
Was/were.
(See activities for **is + verb + -ing** as in Activity 3 above).
Was and **were** denote the past continuous tense. Activate the dolls as described for is/was, but make a show of removing them from behind the barrier and indicating that they have completed their activities before asking the question:
'Was/were the boy(s) sleeping?'

Can, will, may + verb: can go, will come

Activity 1:

Target:
Can (meaning able – I can open the box).

Materials:
Objects placed out of reach on a cupboard, a piece of string, a doll too large to fit into a model car, some broken objects.
a) Ask the child to reach for an object on the cupboard. Discuss this together:
'You can/can't reach.'
b) Tie knots in the piece of string – some tighter than others. Take turns undoing them while you discuss the activity:
'I can undo it.'
'I can't. Can you?'
c) Tell the child to place the doll inside the car:
'Can it fit? It can't! It's too big.'
d) Tell the child to 'fix' the broken objects. Discuss:
'Its broken. I can/can't fix it!'
(See also the Negative.)

Activity 2:

Target:
Can (meaning it's possible – can fish fly?)

Materials:
None.
Ask the child questions:
'Can balls eat?'
'Can dogs bark?'
Encourage him to reply in a full sentence:
'No, balls can't (eat).'

Note:
Can (seeking permission) – Can I go?
This question does not develop until a later stage (see Interrogative Reversals).

Activity 3:

Target:
Will (to denote future tense: Tomorrow I will go).

Materials:
Toys such as a puzzle, a posting box and shapes, a mechanical toy. It is important to contrast future tense with present or past tense. Place the toys in order. Ask the child:
'What will you do first?'
'I will (do the puzzle).'
'What will you do next?'
'I will wind up (the mouse).'
Then allow him to act. While doing so encourage him to tell you:
'I'm doing (the puzzle).'
Having completed the activities he may then tell you:
'I did (the puzzle).'

Activity 4:

Target:
Will do (to denote intention: I will sit and wait).

Materials:
A puppet, sweets or raisins, a cup of water, a bag of blocks or tokens.
Tell the child:
'This puppet is naughty. You tell him: Don't (eat the sweets!), don't (spill the water!).'
Allow the child to activate the puppet and speak for him:
'I will (eat the sweets!).'
Contrast **will** with the negative **won't** (see the Negative).

Note:
May: this structure has been omitted as it is seldom used by children.

Obligatory do + verb: don't go

According to Lee (1974) **do** emerges before the forms **did** and **does** in normal child language development. **Do** should be taught in contrast to the negative – **don't**. Be careful not to use the question form at first – it develops at a later stage (see Negatives and Interrogative Reversals).

Activity 1:

Target:
Do/don't (obligatory do + verb).

Materials:
Attractive toys and objects.
Offer these to the child one at a time, asking him:
'Do you want (the watch)?'
Assist him to reply:
'I do/don't.'
Don't reverse roles as he is unlikely to be able to use the question form at this stage.

Activity 2:

Target:
Do/don't (obligatory do + verb).

Materials:
None. Ask questions such as:
'Do dogs bark? Do trees eat?' Model the response if necessary:
'They do/don't.'

Emphatic do: do + verb

When **do** receives stress, this adds exclamatory emphasis to the whole sentence:

I **do** see. You **do** look ill.

Activity 1:

Target:
Did/didn't.

Materials:
Tupperware blocks or boxes of varying colours; small objects or toys.
Take turns hiding or removing the object from the boxes. The seeker must then ask:
'Did you take it from/put it in the red/blue/yellow box?'
Reply:
'I did/didn't...'

Activity 2:

Target:
Do/don't.

Materials:
Lotto – share out the large sheets of pictures.
As you display picture card by picture card, say to the child:
'You don't want the (cot).'
When you name a card which he does in fact need to complete his sheet, assist him to say:
'I do want (it).'

Variation:

Use every opportunity during your sessions to withhold a desired object from the child. Say:
'You don't want/like (this).'
He must be encouraged to reply:
'I do want/like (it).'

Could, would, should, might +verb

Note:
The negative forms couldn't, wouldn't etc. develop later than the positive.

Activity 1:

Target:
Could/might (possibility – what could/might happen).

Materials:
Story sequence cards.
Present the cards in order as you tell the story, but omit the final card. Ask:
'What could/might happen next?'
Reply:
'(The boy) could (eat the cake).'

Variation:

Present a single card depicting an event and ask:
'What could/might happen next?'

Activity 2:

Target:
Could (ability – he could stand on the chair).
Would (probability – he would fall off).

Materials:
If required, use model dolls and objects to illustrate your questions.
Ask the child questions such as:
'Could a buck live in the lion's cage?'
Reply:
'No, the lion would eat it.'
'I could put the man on the house.'
'No, he would fall off.'
Reverse roles, allowing the child to manipulate the pictures or objects using the target utterance.

Activity 3:

Target:
Can/could (permission – could I go?).
(See Interrogative Reversals, and the Negative.)

Materials:
A puzzle.
Ask one another:
'Can/could this piece (of puzzle) fit here?'
Reply:
'Yes/no it can/can't/could/couldn't.'

Activity 4:

Target:
Would (implying characteristic activity – Which one would you use?)

Materials:
Pictures or objects – tools, kitchen utensils, cutlery, etc.
Ask:
'Which one would you use to stir the soup/to hammer a nail?'
Target utterance:
'I would use the spoon/hammer.'

Note:
Would may be used in other contexts which include:
a) **A characteristic activity**: Every day he would go to the shop.
b) **Willingness**: Would you mind?
c) **Insistence**: You would keep doing that.
These may be used in narration or discourse in order to expose the child to such structures.

Activity 5:

Target:
Should (most commonly used by children as obligation and logical necessity – You should do that!)
Ask questions with a social/moral content:
'Should people steal?'
'Should we drive very fast?'
Target response:
No/yes we shouldn't/should.

Note:
You may extend this to asking:
'Why?'
'Because...'

Obligatory does, did + verb

See **obligatory do** for explanation and activities. Substitute the 3rd person singular by referring to an animal, doll or puppet in all activities for the target form **does**:
He does want an apple.

Activity:

Target:
Did.

Materials:
Model vehicles, cooking utensils or tools.
Close your eyes while the child acts with one of the objects: pushes a car/stirs with a spoon. Ask:
'Did you (stir with the spoon)?'
Target response:
I did/didn't.
Reverse roles so that the child uses the question form.

Emphatic does, did, +verb

See **obligatory do**. Substitute the 3rd person singular by referring to an animal, doll or puppet in all relevant activities for target form **does**: He does go.

Activity:

Target:
Did.
Use the activity described in **obligatory does** for teaching **did**.
Run through all the possible actions the child could have made by stating emphatically:
'You didn't push the car/stir with a spoon.'
When you come to the correct choice, he replies:
'I did.'
Reverse roles so that the child uses the negative form.
(See also Questions: Where does/did?)

Passive with get, any tense
Passive with be, any tense

Always use the Active Voice as a contrast.

Activity 1:

Target:
Passive with **be**.

Materials:
Model dolls to act as the subjects of the sentence; model objects such as fruit, a horse, a bicycle to act as the objects of the sentence. Activate the models appropriately in the active voice:
'Daddy cuts the apple.'
Now reverse subject and object indicating the absurdity of the statement:
'The apple cuts Daddy.'
Model the correct form in the passive voice:
'The apple is cut by Daddy.'
Varying the lexical items, start the sentence and assist the child to complete the target utterance:
'The banana...(is eaten by Mommy).'
'The orange...(is squeezed by the girl).'
'The horse....(is ridden by the boy).'
Now assist the child to complete the sentence on his own. You may cue him by pointing first to the object to remind him it comes before the subject in this structure. Remember to vary the tense, using past, present and future tenses appropriately.

Activity 2:

Target:
Passive with **got**.
Activate the models as used in Activity 1, but the subjects must now be seen to receive or fetch the objects:
Daddy got the apple. The apple was got by Daddy.

Note:
Remember that we are following the natural progression of child language, even if this sounds somewhat offensive to proficient English speakers!

Must, shall + verb: must come

Activity:

Target:
Must.

Materials:
None. Allow the child to be 'teacher'. He instructs dolls (or classmates):
'You must touch your toes/pick up the paper.'

Have + verb + -en: I've eaten

Activity:

Materials:
Household objects.
The child acts out activities: he brushes his teeth, stirs an imaginary soup, sweeps the floor. On completion, assist him to use the target utterance appropriately:
'I have brushed my/teeth/ stirred the soup/ swept the floor.'
Now close your eyes while he completes only a few of the activities. Ask: 'Have you brushed your teeth/stirred the soup?'

Variation:
Allow the child to manipulate dolls to carry out the activity in order to use the 3rd person: He has/hasn't...

Have got: I've got it

Activity:

Materials:
A variety of objects.
Place the objects between you and name each one. Close your eyes while the child removes one object. Then guess:
'Have you got a (cup)?'
Reply:
'I have/haven't (got a cup)'.
You may use the utterance:
'Who has got my (spoon)?'
Reverse roles so the child asks the question. This game is more meaningful if there is a group of children.

Variation:

Use the game of lotto.
Display each picture and ask:
'Have you got the (shoe)?'
Reply:
'No, I haven't got (the shoe).'

Have been + verb + -ing
Had been + verb + -ing

Activity 1:

Materials:
Several toys or activities.
Instruct the child to select a single toy and play with it while you briefly leave the room or busy yourself with something. On returning ask: 'What have you been doing?'
Reply:
'I've been playing (with the puzzle).'
'Have you been playing with the puzzle or have you been playing with the train?'
Reverse roles so that the child asks the question.

> ### Activity 2:
> **Materials:**
> Sequence stories.
> Tell the story, using the target form:
> The boy had been playing in the garden, when his mother called him.
> Encourage the child to use the target utterance when telling you the story. Use the forced alternative as described in Activity 1, and elicit the question form as well as the negative:
> 'Had the boy been digging on the beach?'
> 'No, he hadn't.'

Modal + have + verb + -en

May have eaten.

Modal + be + verb + -ing

Could be playing.

Other auxiliary combinations

Should have been sleeping.

Select your target utterance and use it liberally when telling a story. Language-impaired children are inclined to omit auxiliaries and modals, and they will require frequent prompting in spontaneous speech. Remember that the pragmatic use of language is the most relevant teaching context. Do not rely on teaching written forms in a rote fashion in the hope that these complex verb phrases will be acquired.

Activities to teach secondary verbs

Five early-developing infinitives

Activity 1:

Target:
Let me (lemme).

Materials:
Any activity necessitating 'turn-taking' – a kaleidoscope or viewmaster is fun to use here.
Take turns to view the pattern, using the target utterance:
Let me (see).

Variation:

Target:
Let's.

Materials:
Any activity necessitating working together – building blocks, drawing materials.
Build a construction while using the target utterance:
Let's (draw a house).
Encourage the child to use the target utterance appropriately.

Activity 2:

Target:
Got to (gotta).

Materials:
A map of a town drawn on cardboard (see the chapter on Equipment in Book Two); model dolls and vehicles.
Take turns in manipulating the toys on the map using the target utterance: 'Mommy's got to go down the road/to the shop/home.'

Non-complementing Infinitives:

I stopped to play.
I'm afraid to look.

Activity :

Target:
I like to....., I want to...

Materials:
A selection of foods (use picture cards), a selection of activities.
Take turns using the target utterances appropriately:
a) **like** – I like to eat (bananas). I don't like to eat (apples).
b) **want** – I want (to do the puzzle). I don't want (to play with the car).

Variation:

Select a variety of non-complementing infinitives – use them repeatedly while telling sequence stories. Elicit these from the child by using the forced alternative:
'Does the boy want to ride his bike or does he want to go for a swim?'

Participle, present or past

I see a boy running.
I found the toy broken.

Activity 1:

Target:
Present participle

Materials:
Action picture cards.
Having described each card, share them between the 'players'. Hold them as playing cards ensuring that the 'opponent' cannot see them. Ask one another:
'Have you got the boy running (the girl skipping)?'
If the answer is 'yes', the questioner may keep the card.

Activity 2:
Target:
Past participle
Materials:
Pictures or models of people.
Take turns in naming each individual:
'This boy is named (John).'

Infinitive complements

Early infinitival complements with differing subjects in kernels:
> I want you to come

Activity:
Materials:
None.
Alternate roles as teacher and pupil while you and the child use the target utterance:
'I want you (to pick up the chalk/walk to the window).'

Later infinitive complements

I had to go.
I told him to go.
I tried to go.
He ought to go.

Activity:
Materials:
The town map as used for **got to** (early-developing infinitives).
Assist the child to use the appropriate forms of the infinitive as he manipulates the models:
'Mommy has to go to the shop.'
'I'm telling the girl to go to school.'

Obligatory deletions

Make it (to) go.
I'd better (to) go.

Activity:
Materials:
A wind-up toy or model car; coloured blocks.
Instruct one another to:
'Make the car (it) go to the red block/behind the green block, quickly.'

Note:
A second adverbial has been added to the target (LARSP:XYAA).

Passive infinitival complement, with get
I have to get dressed.
I don't want to get hurt.

Passive infinitival complement, with be
I want to be pulled.
It's going to be locked.

Activity:
Materials:
A model doll, clothing and furniture, or sequence pictures of a child going through a dressing and eating routine.
Model as you manipulate the objects or describe the pictures:
'First she has to get up. Then she has to get dressed.' etc.
Assist the child to use the target utterances along with you.

Variations:
Select any of the target utterances and construct a relevant situation in order to use it repeatedly, making sure that the child is also enabled to use it appropriately. For example:
'I want to be pulled/pushed.'
Use a tricycle or wagon and manipulate the vehicle as he demands:
'I want to be pushed.'
'I don't want to be pushed.'

Gerund

Swinging is fun.
I like fishing.
He started laughing.

Activity 1:

Target:
I like don't like / eating / fishing / coming to school.
Discuss with the child what he does and doesn't like doing:
'I don't like coming to school. I like swimming.'

Activity 2:

Materials:
Pictures of household implements or tools.
Ask:
'What is a broom/knife for?'
Reply:
'For sweeping/cutting.'

4. The Negative

Throughout our lesson plans we have given attention to the teaching of the negative form. In accordance with our principle of teaching structures by contrast, negatives can be included at every stage of therapy in conjunction with work on any structure. As we have seen, the development of negative verbs is dependent on the development of the auxiliary, and thus until Stage IV negativisation takes place outside the sentence. Not only verbs, however, can be negated. Negativisation applies to other forms such as:

Adverbs: never, nowhere.

Pronouns: nothing, no one.

Quantifiers: no more

The negative morpheme **not** is placed after the first auxiliary verb to form the negative in the verb phrase. The negative interrogative **not** is placed after the ordinary interrogative:
    Didn't (did not) you see her?
    Isn't (is not) he coming?

(See LARSP Stage IV, Neg V, Book Two.)

Children's development of negation with verbs

Menyuk (1971, p.73) records the development sequence as follows:

Modal	*Copula*	*Auxiliary*
No do this	No cowboy	No touch
I no do this	That not cowboy	I not touch
I can't do this	That's not a cowboy	I'm not touching

Bloom (1970) relates negative development to semantics. Firstly, the negative is used as a statement of non-existence of an object or action.

>No Daddy – meaning: Daddy's not here.

Secondly, it is used as a means of rejection:

>No milk – meaning: I don't want milk.

Finally, the negative implies denial:

>No break – meaning: I didn't break it.

Note that **not** is used at a later stage.

When children begin to use sentences, other forms of negation appear:

>Can't, don't, won't, isn't.

Can't and **don't** are probably heard so often by children that they learn them as 'giant' words and not as the negative forms of **can** and **do** (Lee 1974).

Problems encountered with the negative

Children may not understand the meaning of the negative unless it is contrasted with the positive. For this reason all activities suggested in this text include such formally contrastive activities. Some children do not easily make the transition **no** to **not** in the verb phrase, and hearing-impaired children may find this particularly difficult.

Lee (1974) suggests attaching the negative to the first auxiliary by use of elliptical sentences:

>He can't! I won't!

This is easier for the child than using the whole sentence:

>He cannot come today. I will not go there.

Activities to teach the negative

It, this, that and the copula or auxiliary is, 's and not:

It's not mine.
This is not a dog.
This is not moving.

(See all activities for **it, this** and **that** – Indefinite Pronouns; **is, 's**- copula and **is + -ing** – Main Verbs.)

Can't, don't

(See **can**, **obligatory** and **emphatic do** – Main Verbs.)

Isn't , won't

(See **copula** and **auxiliary is** and **will** – Main Verbs.)

All other negatives

Uncontracted negatives

I can not go.
He has not gone.
(See **can** and **have** – Main Verbs.)

Pronoun – auxiliary or pronoun – copula contraction

I'm not coming.
He's not here.
(See Copula, Auxiliary Main Verbs, and Pronouns.)

Auxiliary – negative or copula – negative contraction

He wasn't going.
He hasn't been seen.
It couldn't be mine.
They aren't big.

All the relevant main verbs should be contrasted with their negative forms where appropriate.

5. Questions

Questions are requests for confirmation or information. They are a very important part of discourse, as children may use them to maintain conversation, to explore the environment, to learn new words, and to glean information.
Questions may take the form of interrogative reversals (yes/no questions) or wh-questions.

The interrogative question

These questions seek affirmation or negation. There are four ways to ask yes/no questions:

1) Variation of intonation
The pitch of the voice rises at the end of an utterance:
>You want an apple?

2) Inversion
The utterance begins with an auxiliary or copula instead of the subject of the sentence:
>Have you got my book?
>Is it red?
>Are they coming?

3) Do Insertion
Do is used in place of the auxiliary or copula, and will denote tense:
>Do you want it?
>Did he come?

4) Tag questions
A statement is made and then a request follows to check if it is true. Early forms are pre-tags:
>You're coming, huh?

True tags involve the use of an auxiliary or **do**:
>You do want it, don't you?
>You will see me, won't you?
>(Lund and Duchan 1983; Lee 1974; Miller 1981; Crystal *et al.* 1976).

The development of the interrogative reversal

Much has been said about the teaching of the auxiliary, and this is all linked to the teaching of verb inversion. Questions are first marked by rising intonation only:

> See car? (Do you see my car?)

Menyuk (1971, p.73) records the development of the yes/no question form as follows:

Copula	*Auxiliary*
This powder?	Make it?
This is powder?	He's make it?
Is this is the powder?	Does he make it?
Is this the powder?	Is he making it?

The auxiliary and copula begin to be used and appropriately inverted at about 3 years of age.

Teaching yes/no questions

Lee (1974) suggests that the yes/no question is closely associated with the negative. She introduces questions in a game involving the non-existence of an object:

In our programme, you will notice that all activities are designed to teach the question, statement, positive and negative simultaneously. However,

> No crayon
> Crayon? No. Draw?
> Draw a picture? No. No crayon.
> Want a crayon?

some of these forms do develop later than others, so be careful to adjust your therapy as we have suggested.

(For Interrogative Reversals and Yes/No Questions see Main Verbs.)

Wh-Questions

These questions seek information, and are formed by placing a specific question word at the beginning of the sentence. These words are:
Who (be), **what, where, which, how** and **when.**
The word is the key to the information the speaker is attempting to glean:
Where? (location), **when**? (time), etc.
The wh word may also be found in the position of missing information:

> Gary, will do what?

Some wh-questions occur together with yes/no questions as in:

> Know where my shoes are?

(Brown 1973, cited by Lund and Duchan 1983.)
(See section on Conjunctions and Personal Pronouns.)

Remember children may confuse the use of wh-questions with personal pronouns or conjunctions when the same lexical item is involved:

> I know how I can go (Conjunction).
> How can I go? (Wh-question).
> I know what I want (Personal Pronoun).
> What do I want? (Wh- question).

228

The development of wh-questions

18 months – 2 years. Stage I:

The wh word is combined with a single element or noun phrase:
>What that?
>What he do?

2 years – 28 months. Stage II:
>**What NP** (doing)
>**Where NP** (go):
>What man doing?
>Where horse go?

29 – 30 months. Stage III:

Appearance of novel wh-questions:
>**What + (N) + V**
>**Where +(N) + V**:
>What getting?
>Where he going?
>What book name?
>Where: NP + (VP) + (NP)
>Where my coat?
>Why you cross?

31 – 34 months. Stage IV:

Auxiliary appears but is not inverted:
>Why I can't have it?
>Where the book is?
>Why you smack me?

Stage V:

The **auxiliary** is appropriately **inverted**:
>**Aux + NP + VP**:
>Where is the glass of milk?

The auxiliary may include: are, can, will and do.

(Lund and Duchan 1983; Miller 1981; Menyuk 1971; Crystal *et al*. 1976.)

Miller (1983, p.46) lists the wh-questions and the information they elicit:

What –	What is that?(object) Response: A (ball).
What do –	What are you doing? Response: Jumping.
Where –	Where is it? (location) Response: Under the table.
Where –	Where did he go? (direction) Response: To town.
Whose –	Whose hat is this? (possessor) Response: His!
Who –	Who is home? (person) Response: All the children.
Why –	Why are you crying? (reason or cause) Response: Because I fell.
How –	How can I eat this? (manner or instrument) Response: With a spoon.
When –	When did he come? (time) Response: Yesterday.
How many	How many do you want? (number) Response: Four.
How much	How much rain did you have? (amount) Response: Not much.
How long	How long must we wait? (duration) Response: Until I come.
How far	How far is Durban? (distance) Response: Forty–five kilometres.
How often	How often do you see him? (frequency) Response: Every Friday.

Some relevant points to remember when teaching the wh-question:

1) Be sure your activity is realistic. The questioner must legitimately require the relevant information. If you expect the child to ask 'what?'(object), he must be unable to see or identify the object in question. If you want him to ask 'how many?', he must be unable to ascertain the number himself. He must comprehend the logical causality between 'why' and 'because', and must ask 'how' to discover the manner in which an event occurred, or the instrument used to carry it out.

2) Some children have great difficulty learning discourse. They may echo the questions you ask instead of replying to them. There are several techniques to use in order to encourage turn-taking. Place your fingers lightly on the child's lips indicating he is to be quiet – it's your turn. Break eye contact with him while you speak, and then look directly at him when you expect his reply. Reverse roles and use props in order to reinforce role differentiation. (See activities to teach the Copula and Auxiliary **is** – Main Verbs.)

Remember there is a progression of development for this language form, so don't expect correct word order or a complete utterance at first. (See LARSP – Question Development.)

Activities to teach wh-questions

Note that in all these activities you need to act as questioner first, so as to model the target utterance.

Who, what, what + noun

Who am I?
What is he eating?
What book are you reading?
(See activities to teach **somebody**, **something**, **nobody**, **nothing**, Indefinite Pronouns.)

Activity 1:

Target:
Who? what?

Materials:
Doll family, a variety of objects, two containers – A & B.
Assist the child in placing a doll into a container A, but indicate that you did not see which doll was selected. Ask:
'Who ('s) in?'
If he does not respond, guess:
'Is it Mommy?'
When he names the doll or reveals it to you, be very careful not to echo the name. Simply reply:
'Oh!'
and take the doll. You are discouraging echolalia and encouraging discourse. Reverse roles. Wait in silence expectantly for his question: 'Who?'
If he doesn't ask this, say (or gesture):
'You ask me: "Who?".'
When he uses the target utterance be sure to reveal the doll immediately.
Play the same game with the objects and container B. This time the target is
'What?'(objects).
When he's using both 'who' and 'what' appropriately, alternate hiding a doll and an object in the appropriate containers.

Note: Be sure you keep the objects in the appropriate containers, so that container A elicits the question 'who' and container B elicits the question 'what'. It is hoped that the child will begin to comprehend the difference and appropriate use of these two wh-questions.

Variations:
Use **what** and **who** with a variety of prepositions:
Who/what is on/in/under/behind?

Activity 2:

Target:
Who? what?
Who/what('s) that?

Materials:
Pictures of people; pictures of objects.
Identify all the cards. Share out the pictures of people. Each player holds up a card with its back to the 'opponent'. Guess – who is on the card?
'Who('s) that? Is it (Mommy?)'
Now share out the pictures of the objects and use the target utterance: 'What ('s) that?' (See activities to teach the Copula **is** – Verbs.)

Activity 3:

Target:
What + noun.

Materials:
3 model cars differing in colour. 2 model horses – one large and one small; several tokens, differing in colour.
Use the model cars. Assist the child to hide one of the cars behind his back. Ask:
'What car is that? Is it the red car?'
When you have guessed correctly, reverse roles so the child uses target question.

Variations:
Vary the objects (nouns) by using the horses or tokens.
'What horse is that? The big horse?'
'What colour is that? Red?'

Activity 4:

Target:
Who.

Materials:
Various small objects – a cent, a button.
This activity is best used in a group. Place all the objects before you. Close your eyes while each child takes an object. Then ask:
'Who's got the (cent)?'
Guess:
'Is it (Kenny)?'
Each child may have a turn to act as seeker/questioner while trying to locate the objects.

Activity 5:

Target:
Who? what?

Materials:
A picture of a scene in which several people are acting – a park, a beach.
Ask the child questions:
'Who's swimming?'
'What's sailing?'
'Who's running?'
' What's flying?'
His response will indicate that he understands the difference between **who** and **what**, particularly if you use the same verb:
'Who's swimming?'
Response:
'Children.'
'What's swimming?'
Response:
'A fish.'

Where, how many, how much, what...do, what...for

Where did it go?
How much do you want?
What is he doing?
What is a hammer for?

Activity 1:

Target:
Where?

Materials:
A single object.
Assist the child to hide the object, pretending not to see where he's put it. (It does help to have two adults participating in this game at first.) Ask:
'Where's (the ball)?'
He may show you rather than tell you at this stage. Reverse roles so that he uses the target question.

Activity 2:

Where did/does?

Materials:
A model farm/dolls' house.
Take turns placing the models in selected areas by asking one another: 'Where does the Daddy/horse go?'
Reply:
'In the bathroom/ in the barn/ on the chair/ behind the cow' etc.
By making this a guessing game, with one 'player' closing his eyes whilst the other places the models, the target becomes:
'Where did the Daddy/horse go?'
You may also use the question form:
'Where does the daddy/cow belong?'
For the slightly older child with a well developed sense of the absurd you can have some fun drawing people with body-parts misplaced:
'Where does the nose belong? On his leg!'

Activity 3:

Target:
How many/how much?

Materials:
Counters, buttons, coins – commensurate with the number he can count.
Assist the child to hide a few (counters) behind his back. Ask him:
'How many?'
His response:
'(Two).'
Reverse roles so that he asks the target question.

Variations:
Use the coins to elicit the target:
How much (money?)

Note:
This may be incorporated into a game of 'shopping' if the child is old enough to understand imaginative games.

Activity 4:
'What (is/was the boy doing)?'

Materials:
Model person (you may use the children themselves if you are working in a group); model furniture or other household objects, a barrier.
As in the games described to teach the auxiliaries (see the Verb), encourage the child to activate the model behind the barrier, or allow a child in the group to act while the others close their eyes.
Use the target utterance to ask:
'What is the boy/Daniel doing?'
Then guess:
'He's drinking (from the cup)/ He's cutting (the apple)/ He's standing (on the chair)' etc.
Reverse roles so that the child uses target utterance.

Activity 5:

Target:
What (will happen next)?

Materials:
Sequence story cards.
Take turns telling the story by card, but the narrator places the last card, which illustrates the outcome of the story, upside down. He must then ask the listener:
'What will happen next?'

Activity 6:

Target:
What (do you feel)?

Materials:
A soft bag with objects of varying shapes and textures. Allow the child to feel an object through the bag. Ask him:
'What do you feel?'
His response should be:
'Something soft/long/furry', etc.
Reverse roles so that he uses the target utterance.
You may include other questions such as **what + noun**:
'What toy is that?' (he must know the contents of the bag to guess the answer).

Activity 7:

Target:
What...do?

Materials:
Picture cards of a single subject acting – a boy swinging, a boy climbing. Do not vary the subject – this introduces too many variables.
Describe the pictures, then turn them all face downwards. Take turns selecting a picture. The other player must guess:
'What ('s) the boy doing? Jumping/climbing?'

Variations:
1) Use a model doll and furniture.
(See activity to teach **is + ing** – Main Verbs.)
The target is not: Is the boy (bathing)? but:
What is the boy doing? Bathing?
2) You or the child may act, while the other closes his/her eyes:
What are you doing? Writing/walking?

Activity 8:

Target:
What...for?

Materials:
Objects such as a toothbrush, a comb, a spoon, a hammer, a pencil.
You may use pictures of the objects and ask:
'What's (a brush) for?'
Response:
'Brushing your hair.'

Variation:
The child hides one object behind his back. Ask him:
'What ('s that) for?'
Response:
'(To) brush (your) hair.'
You then guess:
'It's a (brush!)'
Reverse roles.

When, how, how + adjective

When shall I come?
How do you do it?
How big is it?

Activity 1:

Target:
When?

Materials:
A model farmyard.
Line up all the animals to be fed, but keep several aside. Let the child 'feed' the animals and ask him:
'When can the (pig) eat?'
Response:
'Now/ later/after the duck/before the cow.'
Let him select the animals to be excluded so that he can ask you when they may be fed.

Variation:

Use any model scene necessitating turn-taking by the participants:
'When can I push the car?'
'When can the girl swing?'

Activity 2:

Target:
How?

Materials:
None. Ask:
'How do you jump/dance/hop.'
The child needs to understand that he must demonstrate these activities.

Variation:

Ask:
'How does a bird fly?'
'How does an elephant drink?'
If the child is unable to supply a verbal response, he may demonstrate.

Activity 3:

Target:
How.

Materials:
Models or pictures to demonstrate the following:
Question: How can the boy reach the biscuit jar?
Response: He must climb on the chair.
Question: How can we mend this toy?
Response: With glue.
Question: How does Mommy go to the shop?
Response: In a bus.
Question: How does Father Christmas get into our house?
Response: Down the chimney.

Variation:

Use absurd solutions to amuse the child and increase his cognitive awareness of this structure.

Materials:
Pictures or objects to illustrate the following:
Question: How can I cut the paper?
Response: With a shoe.
Question: How can I stir the porridge?
Response: With a hammer.
Question: How does a dog bark?
Response: Meow.
Try to reverse roles, allowing the child to ask the questions.
(He may not be spontaneous enough to do this as yet.)

Activity 4:

Target:
How + adjective.

Materials:
Map of a town (see Equipment – Book One), model cars.
Draw lines across a road at regular intervals. Manipulate the car on the road and ask:
'How **far** must I go?'
The response:
'There/ to that line/ to the shop.'
Ask:
'How **fast** must I go?'
Response: (This will probably be in the form of a demonstration by the child).
Reverse roles so that he uses the target utterance.

Variations:
Build a block tower and ask:
'How high (must I build it)?'
Build a block train and ask:
'How long must I make it?'
Share out objects or sweets and ask:
'How many do you want?'

Why, what if, how come, how about + gerund

Why are you crying?
What if I won't do it?
How come he is crying?
How about coming with me?
Why?

(See **because** – Conjunctions. At this stage assist the child to ask the question as well as being able to supply the response.)

> **Activity:**
>
> **Target:**
> What if....?
>
> **Materials:**
> Objects or pictures to illustrate the following:
> a) Assist the child to build a block tower. Pretend to pull out the bottom block. Ask:
> 'What if I pull this out?'
> Response:
> '(Then) all the blocks will fall.'
> b) Attempt to insert buttons too large for a slit in a bottle-lid. Ask:
> 'What if I take off the lid?'
> Response:
> '(Then) the buttons could go in.'
> c) Pour water into a container. Pretend you will keep on pouring even when its full. Ask:
> 'What if I pour more water?'
> Response:
> '(Then) it will spill.'
> If the child is sufficiently spontaneous, assist him to make up some 'what ifs' of his own.

How about

This structure is best demonstrated during the day's activities:

'How about painting a picture/playing outside.'

How come

This is not frequently used by South African English speakers.

Whose, which, which + noun

Be careful that the child does not confuse these with personal pronouns:
    I know whose this is (personal pronoun).
    Whose is this? (wh-question).
    I can't choose which book to read (personal pronoun).
    Which book shall I choose? (wh-question).

Activity 1:

Target:
Whose?

Materials:
Pictures of objects which are character specific: a fireman's hat, a doctor's stethoscope, a farmer's tractor, a man's shirt, a woman's shoe, a baby's bottle.
Indicating one picture at a time ask:
'Whose (hat) is this?'
Response:
'A fireman's.'
Reverse roles so that the child uses the target utterance.
If you are working with a group, you may collect possessions from each member. Then ask:
'Whose (hat) is this? Whose (case) is this?'
Allow each child to be 'teacher' in order to use the target utterance.

Activity 2:

Materials:
Two balls, two sweets, two cars, two tokens etc.
Indicating the two balls ask:
'Which do you want?'
Response:
'That one.'
Share out all the objects in this manner, allowing the child time to enjoy playing with the toys of his choice. Reverse roles so that he uses the target utterance.

Activity 3:

Target:
Which + noun.
Use activity 2, but alter the target utterance:
Which ball do you want?

Variation:

Materials:
2 balls differing in size, 2 different kinds of sweets, 2 dolls.
Indicating the two balls ask: Which (ball) is the biggest?
Indicating the two sweets ask: Which (sweet) is the nicest?
Indicating the two dolls ask: Which (doll) is the prettiest?

6. Conjunctions

Complex sentence formation occurs when two or more clauses are bound together, or one clause is embedded in another.

As illustrated on the LARSP (Stage V – Book Two), conjunctions are connecting devices between sentences, the choice of which indicates the relationship between the sentences. The use of one conjunction or another is semantically significant, and in order to convey the appropriate meaning between the sentences, the correct conjunction must be selected (Pink and Thomas 1970; Crystal 1982; Lee 1974).

The Development of Conjunctions in Children

Recursion refers to the ability to connect sentences together. Language becomes significantly more complex when this stage is reached.

And is usually the first conjunction learned. When children learn concepts of purpose, conditionality and alternative choices, they begin using **so, so that, if** and **or**. Place–time concepts create a need to use wh-conjunctions. **Because** is often used as a single-element stereotyped answer:

Why did you do that? Because!

Wh-pronouns are probably first used as modifiers of objects, as word order remains unchanged in this type of sentence:

That's the boy who I knew.
   (Lee 1974, Crystal *et al.* 1976)

Clinical problems with conjunctions

Lee (1974) lists the following:
   1) The conjunction is omitted:
      Daddy sits down (while) the boy goes to play.
   2) Semantic confusion occurs:
      He went to school so he forgot his case at home.
   3) Syntactic rules are confused: wh-questions are substituted for wh-pronouns and word order is reversed:
      I know who are those children.

Activities to teach Conjunctions

And

(LARSP V Conn. Coord)

Activity 1:

Materials:
Doll family, model furniture.
Place two dolls in the bath and say:
'Mommy is bathing and Daddy is (also) bathing.'

Note:
Both dolls perform the same activity to obviate confusion. Allow the child to manipulate the dolls using the target utterance.

Activity 2:

Materials:
Model animals or picture cards.
Describe each animal:
'The monkey's got fur and he eats bananas. The cow's got horns and she eats grass.'

Note:
Repeated reference to appearance and diet may assist the child to categorise and imitate your model.

But

(LARSP Conn-c. Coord)
This conjunction is used to combine two statements that contrast with one another.

Activity 1:

Materials:
Model dolls and furniture.
Place the boy in the bath. Leave the girl lying on your table.
Indicate that the girl has been forgotten:
'The boy is bathing but the girl is not.'
Variation:
Place the boy in the bath and the girl on a chair:
'The boy is bathing but the girl is sitting.'

Activity 2:

Materials:
Contrasting picture cards. A girl riding a bicycle and another standing beside her bicycle; an aeroplane flying and another on the ground etc.
Take turns describing a pair of pictures:
'This girl is riding her bicycle, but that girl is not.'
(See Equipment – The Wilson Syntax Program.)

So

(LARSP Conn-c. Coord)

Activity 1:
(Note: In this context **and so** is equated with **and**.

Materials:
Model doll family.
Activate the dolls appropriately and describe:
'Daddy is dancing and so is Mommy.'

> **Variation:**
> Use objects with similar characteristics:
> 'The car is red and so is the bus.'
> Be sure that the child uses the target utterance himself.

> **Activity 2:**
> **So** introducing a clause of result.
> ## Materials:
> Appropriate picture pairs illustrating purpose:
>
> A girl undressing; a girl in the bath.
> **Target utterance:**
> The girl is taking off her clothes so she can bath.
>
> A child opening a jar. The child eating a sweet.
> ## Target utterance:
> The girls opens the jar so she can have a sweet.
>
> A child climbing a ladder. The child picking apples.
> ## Target utterance:
> The boy is climbing a ladder so that he can pick apples.
> Use the picture pairs appropriately, placing the second card in the pile face downward. You can then enjoy 'guessing' the purpose of the first action as you both use the target utterances.

Or

(LARSP Conn c. Coord)
Or denotes a choice between two articles or activities:
Do you want cherries or do you want peaches?
> **Note**: The technique of using the Forced Alternative will develop this structure.

> **Activity 1:**
> ## Materials:
> Toys or tokens.
> Offer the child a choice between two articles:
> You can have the watch or you can have the comb.
> Reverse roles so that he uses the target utterance.

247

Activity 2:
Materials:
Map of a city (see Book One, Equipment) with model dolls.
Manipulate the dolls while you say:
'Mommy will go to the shop or Mommy will go to the park.'
Assist the child to use the target **or**.

If

(LARSP Conn S Subord A)
If introduces a clause in a conditional sentence. The **if** clause may come before or after the main clause:
   If you eat your supper, you can have a sweet.
   Mommy will be cross if I'm home late.

Activity 1:

Materials:
Appropriate picture pairs illustrating consequence:

A child dropping a cup. The cup is broken.
Target utterance:
If you drop the cup, it will break.

A child smacking a dog. The dog biting the child.
Target utterance:
If you smack the dog, it will bite.

A child watering a plant. A large plant flowering.
Target utterance:
If you water a plant, it will grow.

Note: Stick figure drawings will suffice. Use the picture pairs appropriately, turning first one of the pair face downwards, and then the other. The child will first learn to place the **if** clause before the main clause:
If you drop the cup, it will break.
The cup will break if you drop it.

Note:
When the **if** clause is in the present tense the main clause is in the future tense.

Because

(LARSP Conn S Subord A)
Because introduces clauses of reason as a response to the question 'Why?':
He can't go because he is sick.

Activity 1:

Materials:
Appropriate picture pairs illustrating reason/causality.

A mother scolding a child. An empty box.
Target:
Mommy is cross because the boy ate the sweets.

A happy boy. A birthday cake.
Target:
The boy is happy because it's his birthday.

A boy crying. The boy falling.
Target:
The boy is crying because he fell.

Note:
Stick figure drawings will suffice. Use the picture pairs appropriately. Place the second card face downwards, and guess the reason for the response in the first picture. Use the question 'why' to elicit:
'Because...'

Note:
You may use these picture pairs and those described for teaching **so** interchangably, but be careful to use them appropriately:
The girl is taking off her clothes because she wants to bath.
The boy ate all the sweets so his Mommy is cross.

> ### Activity 2:
> **Materials:**
> A large doll to ride in a small car, a piece of string, a puzzle with varied shapes.
> Tell the child to place the doll in the car; use the string to tie two chairs together; place the shapes incorrectly into the puzzle frame. None of these tasks will be possible. Then ask 'Why?':
> The doll can't fit because it's too big.
> The string won't tie because it's too short.
> The shapes won't fit because they're in the wrong place.

Other subordinating conjunctions

Where, when, how, while, whether (or not), till, until, unless, since, before, after, for, as

Comparative conjunctions

(LARSP Stage V Comparative)

As + adjective + as, as if, like, that, than

> ### Activity 1:
> **Target:**
> **Like**: You walk like an elephant does!
>
> **Materials:**
> None.
> Instruct the child using the target utterance:
> 'You bark like a dog (barks)!'
> 'You hop like a rabbit (hops)!'
> Reverse roles so that the child uses the target utterance.

Activity 2:

Target:
Like: That looks like a girl eating.

Materials:
Drawing materials.
Take turns drawing pictures of people carrying out activities and comment appropriately.

Activity 3:

Target:
As + adjective + as, than:
I can jump as high as you.
You walk more slowly than a tortoise.
Select activities that will elicit the target utterance from the child. Some suggested games may include:
Jumping: I can jump as high as/ higher than you.
Walking: I can walk as fast as/ as slowly as/ faster than/ slower than you.
Writing: I can write as quickly as/ quicker than you.

Variation:

Compare objects in terms of quality:
This peach is softer than/ as soft as that one.
This string is longer than/ as long as that one.

Activity 4:

Target:
Until, till: I'll hold this until/ till you get back.

Materials:
Model farmyard.
Create a chain of activities and act these out using the target utterance appropriately:
The cows can't come out of the barn until/till the farmer opens the door.
The farmer can't drive the wagon until/till the horse is harnessed.
The horse won't pull the wagon until/till it's fed.
Use techniques such as the forced alternative or incomplete sentence to elicit the structure from the child. Humour is an invaluable adjunct:
'Is the girl milking the cow until the bucket is full or milking the cow until the bucket is empty?'
'The girl is milking the cow...'

Activity 5:

Target:
When: I will go when you come back.
Use the materials as for Activity 1, but substitute **when**:
'The cows will come out of the barn when the farmer opens the door.'
You may substitute a doll's house:
'Mommy will put baby to bed when he is tired.'

Activity 6:

Target:
While: Hold the cat while I get his milk.
Use the materials as for Activities 4 and 5, but substitute **while** appropriately:
'The cow stands still while the farmer milks her.'

Activity 7:

Target:
Until (till), when and while.

Materials:
Constructive toys.(This activity is suitable for a group.)
Each group member take turns playing 'teacher'. He instructs other group members appropriately:
'Peta, you do the puzzle until I say "stop". Gary, you play with the cars while Kenny builds a tower. Ralph, when Kenny's tower is finished you push it over!'

Activity 8:

Target:
Before and after: The cow jumps after the dog (jumps).

Materials:
Model animals, a barrier.
Activate the animals to jump over the barrier while you and the child use the target utterance appropriately:
The cow (jumps) after the dog jumps.
The horse jumps before the duck (jumps).

Noun clauses introduced by that

(LARSP Stage V Subord O)
I see that you are tired.
You told me that I must come.

Activity:

Materials:
None.
Instruct the child to act:
'Touch your toes.'
'Jump!'
'Fall down!'
Now ask:
'What did I tell you to do?'
Response:
'You told me that I must (jump).'

Note:
This is a somewhat artificial full-sentence response, encouraged so that the child uses the target utterance.

Unless, whether

Activity:

Target:
Unless, whether (or not), if:
Unless you stop, I won't read you a story.
He didn't know whether or not to go.
I wonder if he will pay.
Introduce these structures into sequence stories. Be sure to contrive several opportunities to use them appropriately. Then, using techniques such as the forced alternative and the incomplete sentence, ensure that the child gets an opportunity to use them appropriately.

For

She was upset, for she did not complete her homework.
This structure is not commonly used by children. **Because** is the conjunction usually selected in social contexts.

As

This conjunction is used in many varied semantic contexts, but the young child may limit its use to examples such as those cited below:

Time: Peta came home as Ralph left.
Parallel actions: I danced as I sang.
Reason: We had to take a bus as the car broke down.

Activities:

Materials:
Appropriate pictures or sequence stories illustrating time, parallel actions or reason to demonstrate the above examples.
Encourage the child to describe the picture or narrate the story using **as** appropriately.

Where

(LARSP Conn s Subord A)

Target:
Where: I know where the ball is.

Materials:
Objects to hide.
The child hides the objects about the room. You say:
'I know where (the ball) is. It's under the table behind the curtain.'
When you've guessed the correct locality of all the objects, reverse roles so that the child uses the target utterance.

How

Target:
How: I know how I can go.

Materials:
Drawing materials.
Using stick figure drawings illustrate a sequence story about a boy wanting to cross a river. He may try walking, riding a bike, going by car and finally by boat. The key utterance can be used liberally:
'I know how he can go. He'll go by...'

Obligatory deletions

I run faster than you (run).
I'm as big as a man (is big).
It looks like a dog (looks).

Elliptical deletions

That's why (I took it).
I know how (I can do it).

For activities, refer to the previously described activities, making sure that the second verb is now deleted.

Wh-words and the infinitive

I know how to do it (LARSP Conn s Subord A).
I know where to go.

(See also Personal Pronouns and the Infinitive.)

Activity:

Target:
How to: I know how to bake a cake.

Materials:
None.
Refer to a series of skills, in order to use the appropriate target utterance. Ask:
'Do you know how to do up your shoes/ hop on one leg/ do this puzzle?'
The child is assisted to use the target:
I know how to...

Note:
Using the full sentence is not pragmatically sound. In context the reply would be: I do/ I don't.

7. Adverbs

Adverbs are important parts of language, often neglected in formal language therapy. Work on adverbs involves an elaboration or qualification of the verb phrase.

An adverb is used to qualify a verb, adjective or other adverb. It may also qualify some prepositions and conjunctions. Most prepositions can be used as adverbs.

An adverb has two types of syntactic function: namely, to act as a clause constituent (conjunction), or to modify an adjective or another adverb.

Because of this great heterogeneity of function, the adverb does not fit the definition for other parts of speech. The most common characteristic of the adverb is the suffix **-ly** (see Book Two, Word).

The most common types of adverb have been identified as adverbs of **time**, **place** and **manner**. Other less frequently occurring subcategories may be included under manner, namely:

> *Frequency* (often, always)
> *Certainty* (definitely, probably)
> *Degree* (too, quite)

Adverbials may be:

> *Single words*: The boy came here.
> *Phrases*: The boy went too far (see Prepositions).
> *Clauses*: The boy went as far as he could.

Adverbial clauses have been considered under conjunctions since they are introduced by subordinators (see LARSP Stage V).

The simple form of the adverb (like the adjective) undergoes inflection when there is a comparison involved: fast, faster, fastest (see Word, Book Two).

Adverbs undergo a developmental sequence in child language. Children usually learn adverbs of place first, followed by time and then manner. (Quirk *et al.*1972; Pink and Thomas 1970; Lee 1974; Crystal *et al.* 1976)

Activities to teach the adverb as a single word or phrase

(See also Book Two, Word and **-er, -est, -ly**; see also Prepositions, Conjunctions, Relative Pronouns and Questions in Book Three.)

Adverbs of place

Activity 1:

Target:
Near/far.

Materials:
Model dolls, animals or other objects.
Demonstrate and describe your actions:
'I'm putting the cow near the horse.'
'I'm putting the boy far away in the corner.'
'Mommy – walk far!'

Variation:

Instruct the child:
'Stand near the cupboard.'
'Walk far down the passage.'
Reverse roles so that the child uses the target utterance appropriately.

Activity 2:

Target:
Here/there.

Materials:
Any constructive toy.
Build a construction with the child, using the target utterance and encouraging him to do likewise:
'Put (it)here/there.'
Be sure to preserve the semantic integrity of the target words in terms of distance. You may wish to build two structures together – one beside you and the other at the far end of the room.

Activity 3:

Target:
Up/down.

Materials:
A model vehicle, a sloping surface. Command the vehicles as you manipulate them appropriately:
'Bus – go up/come down.'
(See Verb Part, LARSP, Stage II.)

Variation:

Command one another:
'(Put your) hands up! Fall down!'

Adverbs of time

Now, soon, then, today, tomorrow, after, the next day, next, first, last.

Activity 1:

Target:
Now, today, tomorrow, yesterday.
Teach these items by contrast, and combine them with the activities to teach verb tense (see Main Verbs, above).
Using a calendar depicting days of the week as well as the climate may be of assistance. Discuss:
'Yesterday it was raining.'
'Now we'll have our juice.'
'Tomorrow we'll bake cakes.'

Activity 2:

Target:
Then, after, first, last.

Materials:
Model dolls and household objects.
Demonstrate a sequence of everyday activities using the dolls and objects: First, the boy wakes up. Then he brushes his teeth, and after that he will eat breakfast. His sister wakes up last...
As the child manipulates the equipment ask:
'Who woke first? What did he do then?'

Adverbs of degree

Activity 1:

Target:
Very.

Materials:
A ping-pong ball, a tennis ball, a large gymnastics ball; two doll's dresses varying in size and an adult's dress; two pieces of string measuring several metres and a single piece measuring 2 to 3 centimetres.
Place the balls before the child and describe:
'This ball (tennis ball) is bigger than that one (ping-pong ball).'
'This ball is the biggest (gymnastics ball). It's very big.'
Discuss with the child:
'Which one is the biggest? It's...'
Discuss all the materials appropriately, using the target **very** to apply to the **very** short string, the **very** large dress.

Activity 2:

Target:
Too.
(See **can**, **will**, **may + verb**, Activity 1, in the section on Main Verbs, above.)
Be sure to stress the target **too** where appropriate:
It's too high/hard/small.

Variation:
Use appropriate pictures: a boy trying to reach a tin of biscuits in a cupboard; an adult trying to put on a child's shoe etc.

Adverbs of manner

(See **- ly**, Word, Book Two.)

8. Adjectives

As with adverbs, this grammatical form does not constitute a well defined class. Pronouns, for example **my**, **his** and **this** may also be called adjectives if they are used with a noun:

>My book, his car, this man.

Some features characteristic of adjectives are:

>They can occur in an attributive position, that is, they pre-modify a noun:
>>Big ball.
>
>They can occur in predicative position functioning as a complement:
>>The boy is big.
>
>They can be premodified by the degree adverbs – very, quite, rather and most:
>>The boy is very big.
>
>They can take comparative and superlative forms, by adding -er, -est:
>>That's the biggest boy. He's bigger than Ralph.
>>(See Word, Book Two.)

Adjectives may be categorised as follows:

1) ***Qualitative***: colour, shape, size, texture, weight, 'other':
   A fat boy, a dirty dress.
2) ***Demonstrative***: this, that, these, those: this hat, those shoes.
3) ***Distributive***: each, every, either, neither:
   Every girl is there.
4) ***Quantitative***: some, any, no, few, many, much:
   A few sweets. Numerical designation (five balls).
5) ***Interrogative***: which, what, whose:
   Which apple do you want?
6) ***Possessive***: my, your, his:
   My car
7) ***Relative***:
   Choose whatever colour you like.

When two adjectives of colour are used, they are separated by **and**:

>A red and yellow ball.

When any other two adjectives appear before the noun, they have a definite order in English which must be learnt. Children developing language often make adjectival sequencing errors (LARSP Stage VI).

>We say: a big black cat. (see **Adj Adj N**, Book Two)
>We do not say: a black big cat.

(Pink and Thomas 1970; Quirk *et al.* 1972.)

There are three **degrees of comparison** (see Word, Book Two).

Positive	Comparative	Superlative
dark	darker	darkest
useful	more useful	most useful

Single syllable adjectives form their comparative and superlative by adding **-er** and **-est**.

Adjectives of three or more syllables add the pre-modifiers **more** and **the most**, and adjectives of two syllables follow either one of these syntactic rules.

Irregular comparisons include:

Positive	*Comparative*	*Superlative*
good	better	(the) best
bad	worse	(the) worst
little	less	(the) least
many	more	(the) most
much	more	(the) most
far	further	(the) furthest of (distance and time)
far	farther	(the) farthest of (people and things)
old	older	(the) oldest of (people and things)
old	elder	(the) eldest of (people only)

263

Activities to teach the adjective

Degrees of comparison

> Be sure that the child understands the concepts of positive, comparative and superlative. Using a group of children, call their attention to comparative attributes:
> 'You are the tallest/shortest.'
> 'You have the longest/shortest hair.'
> Compare two children with one another:
> 'Peta is taller/shorter than Gary.'
> 'Kenny's hair is darker/lighter than Ralph's.'
> Ask the children:
> 'Who's bigger/the biggest/ shorter/the shortest?'

When you are sure the child comprehends these concepts, transfer his interest to objects in the environment. Here are some suggestions:

String or sticks: long, longer, longest/ short, shorter, shortest.

Cups or balls: big, bigger, biggest/ small, smaller, smallest.

Block-towers: high, higher, highest/ low, lower, lowest.

Fruits: hard, harder, hardest/ soft, softer, softest.

A pin/pencils: sharp, sharper, sharpest.

Pictures depicting people or objects which are:
      pretty, prettier, prettiest/ ugly, uglier, ugliest.
      fat, fatter, fattest/ thin, thinner, thinnest.

Pictures or models of people who are:
      tall, taller, tallest/ short, shorter, shortest.

Containers filled with water: deep, deeper, deepest (water)/full, fuller, fullest (container)

(see also Book One, Equipment: the 345 Series).

At an appropriate time, introduce irregular comparisons and the more/most forms.

Adjectives of quality

As with degrees of comparison, the first step in teaching these lexical items is to ensure that the child comprehends the concept. He must demonstrate an ability to classify according to quality, as opposed to some other attributes such as function. This is best demonstrated by using adjectives of colour.

Activity:

Materials:
Three model cars (blue, red and yellow); three model balls (blue, red and yellow); three model boats (blue, red and yellow); three model planes (blue, red and yellow).

Place all the objects in groups according to colour – the blue car, the blue ball, the blue boat and so forth. If he is able to imitate you, he is ready to learn colour names. Teach the colour lexicon by introducing one variable at a time:

Step 1: Show the child a red (ball) and name it:
'A red ball. This is red.' (Be sure to use both adjective and noun, so that he does not think the article is 'a red'.)

Step 2: Enjoy identifying and naming other red objects about the room.

Step 3: Introduce a second colour as in Steps 1 and 2: a yellow ball.

Step 4: Place both the red and yellow balls before you. Say:
'(Give me the) red ball.'
If he selects the correct item, let him use the target utterance by holding both balls out to him for selection – he must name the one of his choice.

Step 5: Introduce the noun as a further variable:
     a red ball a red car
     a yellow ball a yellow car

Increase the adjectival and noun variability according to the child's ability. Any adjective of quality may be taught in this contrastive way.

Courtman-Davies (1979, p.135) suggests the use of adjective boxes for storing and sorting objects according to quality. We have found this most useful, as it obviates the necessity for continually procuring appropriate material. Mary Courtman-Davies lists some of the categories under which to store objects:

    1) Hard/soft: pencil, stone, marble, wool, cotton-wool.

    2) Long/short: ribbon, shoe-laces, string, sticks.

    3) Tall/short: containers of various sizes.

    4) Straight/curved: pencils, ruler, a fork, hair clips.

    5) Same/different: mosaic shapes, stickers or 'swop' cards.

    6) Empty/full: containers-full of rice, cereal, stones and some empty containers.

    7) Heavy/light: a feather, a ping-pong ball, cotton wool, stones, a brick.

    8) Open/shut: a paper house with windows and door that will open and shut; a yale lock and key.

    9) Pretty/ugly: plastic monsters, spiders etc., flowers, lace and toy jewellery. (Courtman-Davies comments that this is a difficult box – children and adults don't always consider the same things pretty and ugly!)

    10) Shiny: a mirror, tinfoil, toy jewellery.

    11) Rough/smooth: stones, pebbles, a pot scraper, sandpaper, silk.

    12) Sharp: pins, scissors, a knife.

You may also use pictures to contrast qualities. Photostat a series of simple line drawings (colouring-in books offer a wealth of material).
    Treat the pictures appropriately:
Dirty one copy and leave the other clean:

        a dirty girl/a clean girl
        a dirty book/a clean book

A selection of fresh fruits offers a wealth of descriptive terms: a sticky date, a sweet/juicy orange, a furry peach, a fresh/round/juicy apple, a sour lemon, a prickly pineapple.

9. Prepositions

A preposition expresses a relationship between two things, one of which is represented by the prepositional complement. Place and time are the most common relationships expressed, although there are a variety of other meanings.

A prepositional phrase consists of a preposition followed, usually, by a noun phrase or clause:

>Behind the cupboard.
>From the window to the door.

(See Adverb – phrase and clause.)

Normally a preposition is followed by its complement, but this is not the case when the complement takes first position in the clause, or is absent through ellipses:

>He is so easy to be with.
>That's the car I told you about.

(Quirk *et al.* 1972)

English prepositions may be simple or complex.

1) Simple prepositions

Most prepositions are simple. From a comprehensive list provided by Quirk *et al.* (1972) we have selected those we consider most likely to be used by young children:

>above, across, after, along, around, as, at, before, behind, between, by, down, for, from, in, inside, of, off, on, out, outside, over, past, round, since, than, through, to, under, underneath, until (till), up, with.

2) Complex prepositions

These consist of more than one word. They include:

>as for, along with, out of, away from, on top of, because of, instead of, in front of, onto, into.

Most prepositions may also be used as adverbs, but the adverb is capable of standing alone without the prepositional complement. The adverb is normally stressed, whereas the single preposition is not:

>She ran by (adverb).
>She ran by the river (preposition).
>Kenny ran up (adverb).
>Kenny ran up the street (preposition).
>(Pink and Thomas 1970, p. 11.)

Children's acquisition of prepositions

Menyuk (1971) says that children learn prepositions of place (in the box) before prepositions of time (before you go) and manner (with a hat). They have difficulty determining the correct preposition to use, or they omit it altogether. She gives the example of a child elaborating terms to achieve a finer definition when unable to use the appropriate preposition:

Target:
He gets almost near...
Child's production:
'He gets all the way close to.'

Children may also use prepositions incorrectly because they don't fully understand their meaning:

>'He went outside from the house.'

Teaching prepositions

It is important to teach this grammatical form in several contexts:
>Take the lid off the bottle; take off your shoes; take the ring off the stick; switch off the light.

We favour teaching prepositions and adverbs among the first words introduced to the child (see LARSP Stage I, Book Two).

Remember that at this stage the preposition may stand alone, with the prepositional complement being implied: Off (the table).

Be sure to use fronted objects when teaching such prepositions as **behind** and **in front of**. It is difficult for a child to understand the concept 'in front of (a cup)', as he may not realise that your perspective is different from his, depending upon where you are both seated. Use objects such as model cars, chairs or a cupboard, which have a definite front and back.

Prepositional meanings

The following are some of the ways in which prepositions may be used by young children:

At/to

Destination: He went to Durban.
Place, position: He was at the hospital.
Time: At ten o'clock, at the end, at breakfast, at Christmas.
Compound at may be used with certain adjectives and participles: Good at my work.

By

Place - relative position: He stood by the chair.
Place - relative destination: We went by the old road.
Manner: He went by train.
Passive verbs may be followed by **by**: The window was broken by a stone.

From

Place - position: He came from school; This is my friend from Cape Town.
Time, usually used with **to** or **until (till)**: I'll be here from eight o'clock till ten.
Manner, source or origin: I got it from him.

Since/when/before/after/until/(till)

These lexical items are also used as conjunctions (see Conjunctions, above).

Prepositions of time

I haven't seen it since yesterday.
I went to town before you.
You go after me.
I won't go till the early morning.

269

Away from/off

Place: He took it away from me.
Take off your hat.

On/in/onto/out/out of
To/at/away from

Place: The bee is on the window.
There's a face at the window.

Quirk *et al.* (1972, p. 307) diagrammatically illustrate the relation of meaning between these propositions. Their graphic representation of place and dimension prepositions is a most clinically useful framework.

The contrast between **on** (surface) and **in** (area) is illustrated as follows:

	destination	position	destination	position	
	to	at	(away) from	away from	**DIMENSION-TYPE 0** (point)
	→X	•X	X→	X •	
	on(to)	on	off	off	**DIMENSION-TYPE 1/2** (line or surface)
	in(to)	in	out of	out of	**DIMENSION-TYPE 2/3** (area or volume)
	POSITIVE		**NEGATIVE**		

Figure 7. The relation of meaning between a number of prominent prepositions of place. (From *A Grammar of Contemporary English*, by R. Quirk, S. Greenbaum and J. Svartvik. Longman Group UK Ltd 1972. © Quirk *et al.* 1972.)

Time: Point of time: He came on time
Period of time: Please come in half an hour.

For

Time: Duration: He comes for the holidays.
Manner: Recipient: Do it for me.
Purpose: I'll do it for money.

Above/below/over/under/on top of/underneath/in front of/behind

Quirk *et al.* (1972, p. 311) differentiate these prepositions as describing relative position, relative passage and relative destination.

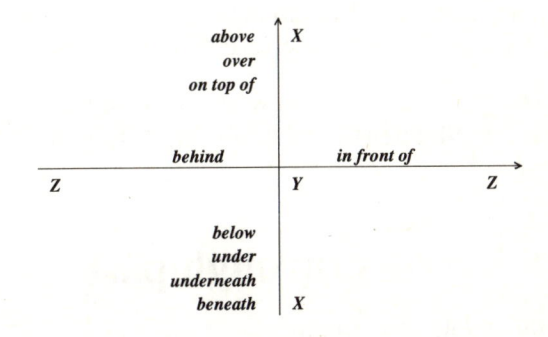

```
                    above    │ X
                    over     │
                    on top of│
                             │
         behind              │     in front of
   Z ────────────────────────┼──────────────────────── Z
                             │ Y
                    below    │
                    under    │
                    underneath│
                    beneath  │ X
```

Figure 8. Vertical and horizontal direction. (From *A Grammar of Contemporary English*, by R. Quirk, S. Greenbaum and J. Swartvik. Longman Group UK Ltd 1972. © Quirk *et al.* 1972.)

Relative position: (Of two objects or groups of objects.)
Examples:

It hangs above the door.
The cover is over the sandpit.
It's behind the curtain.
The car is in front of the garage.
The key is under the mat.
I went behind the tree.
He jumped over the fence.

Note:
Below and **beneath** are not frequently used by young children.

Relative destination: I'll sit on top of the cupboard!
We went underneath the trees.

Above and **below**, **over** and **under**, **in front of** and **behind** are not positive and negative, but converse opposites:

>The picture is above the mantelpiece.
>The mantelpiece is below the picture.
>The bus is in front of the car.
>The car is behind the bus.

Over and **under** as place prepositions are roughly synonymous with **above** and **below** respectively. The main differences are that **over** and **under** tend to indicate a direct vertical relationship and/or spatial proximity, while **above** and **below** may indicate simply on a higher/lower level than:

>The castle stands on a hill above (rather than over) the valley.
>The doctor and the policeman were leaning over (rather than above) the body when we arrived.

Underneath and **beneath** are less common substitutes for **under**; **beneath** is formal in style. **Underneath**, like **on top of**, generally indicates a contiguous relation.

Across/through/past

These prepositions denote movement.

Up/down/along/across/around

Place: These prepositions also express movement. **Up** and **down** denote vertical direction.

Along means from one end towards the other, and **across** means from one side to another in terms of a horizontal axis. **(A)round** means the direction is an angle or a curve:

Examples:
>I ran up/down the stairs.
>Go (a)round the corner.
>Walk along the road.
>Walk across the river.
>**Up** and **down** are also used idiomatically, and imply along:
>He lives up/down the road.

As

Manner: He is as big as me.

(See also Comparative – LARSP V, Book Two.)

Than

Manner: He is bigger than me.

(See also Comparative – LARSP V, Book Two.)

With

Manner: He walks with me.
The man with the hat.

(See Post-modifiers – LARSP Stage V, Book Two.)

Because of

Cause or purpose: He came because of me.

Activities to teach prepositions

Prepositions of place

If we consider a single preposition of place, such as **over**, we find that there are six different meanings designated by it (Quirk *et al*. 1972):

Destination: The aeroplane flew over the town.
Position: The picture hangs over the fireplace.
Passage: He jumped over the log.
Orientation (unlike position, orientation adds a further dimension– the point at which the speaker is standing):They live over the road from us.
Resultative: **over**, when combined with the verb **be**, indicates that the agent has arrived at a destination or state: Gary is over his cold now.
Pervasive: When **over** is preceded by **all** the impression is as follows:
She spilt milk all over her dress.

Therefore, in order to ensure that the child comprehends all the varied meanings of a preposition, be sure to vary your examples and contexts.

Introduce a noun or noun phrase, but keep the preposition constant:
> In/out (of) the box.

Vary the noun when he has mastered this structure:
> In/out (of) the box/basket.

Gradually introduce other prepositions, being sure to contrast them with one another, and to use them in varied contexts.

Activity 1:

Materials:
Climbing apparatus, furniture or cardboard boxes.
Select a single preposition: **in**. Encourage the child to climb in (to) something while you model this preposition in isolation, using signs or gestures to illustrate the meaning. If he is able to follow your command 'In!', encourage him to use the target utterance himself as he stands or goes in (to) a box.
Select a contrasting preposition: **out** (of), and repeat the activity. Now contrast **in** and **out** by using these prepositions alternatively.
Introduce a noun or noun phrase:
In/out (of) the box.
Vary the noun when he has mastered this structure:
In/out (of) the box/basket.
Gradually introduce other prepositions of place, being sure to contrast them with one another, and to use them in varied contexts.
Repeat Activity 1, this time manipulating objects rather than allowing the child to act himself. He needs to comprehend the relation of things in his environment to his own body.

Activity 2:

Materials:
A model map with roads and other features (see Equipment, Book One); model dolls and vehicles; a model farmyard; a garage; blocks with which to construct towers, bridges etc.; planes to fly above or to go up and down. Varying the prepositions or nouns appropriately, you have a wealth of material with which to work:
The car/bus/combi drives up/down/along the road.
The cows/horses/pigs walk/run/in/out of the barn/field.

Activity 3:

Materials:
Pictures depicting the relative position of objects: eg. a ball under/on/being thrown over/a table/chair/cupboard (9 pictures). Place all the pictures before you, being careful to select the variables according to the child's ability. Say:
'The ball is on the chair.'
The child may place tokens on the appropriate picture as you describe it. Reverse roles so that the child uses the appropriate utterance.

Activity 4:

Materials:
A barrier; a duplicate set of objects.
Take turns using the objects to create a structure. Having done so, direct one another to copy this 'creation':
'Put the red block on the yellow block.'
'Put the pig in the blue box and put the blue box on top of the red box.'
'Put the cow by the yellow block.'
Now lift the barrier to see if the two structures are identical.
This is an excellent activity to train the child how to be sensitive to listener context. It is helpful to show him how his incomplete message perplexes you. He may say:
'Put the red block'
or
'Put under the blue block'.
The number of objects used will dictate the degree of complexity.

Prepositions of time
At/in/on

At indicates a fixed point in time: At four o'clock, at dawn,

or idiomatically as in: At birthday celebrations,

in phrases: At all times.

On is used when a particular day is being indicated: On Tuesday, on the following Tuesday.

In indicates periods of time: In the morning, in the April holidays. (Sometimes we say: During the April holidays).

Activity 1:

Target:
On.

Materials:
Make a calendar with large squares representing the days of the week. Allow the children to assist you in illustrating the activities that typically occur on each day–Monday is washing day, Tuesday we play soccer, and so on.
Discuss the events as you select them:
On Sunday, we go to church.

Activity 2:

Target:
In.

Materials:
As in Activity 1, illustrate events that occur: during the seasons, at daytime or night-time. Discuss the events with the children making sure to allow them to contribute spontaneously:
'In the evening–stars shine.'
'In the summer–we swim!'

Activity 3:

Target:
At.

Materials:
A clock with manipulable hands; illustrations of daily events: eating, sleeping, going to school; illustrations of festivals and holidays: New Year, a birthday party etc.
Ask:
'When do we eat breakfast?'
'When does Father Christmas come?'
Assist the child to manipulate the clock or point to the appropriate picture. The response:
'At seven o'clock.'
or
'At Christmas time'.

From/to

Activity 1:

Target:
From.

Materials:
Wind-up toys.
Allow the child to wind up the toy and hold it ready to activate.
Tell him:
'Wait! Not yet. All right, let it go from now.'
Reverse roles so that he uses the target utterance.

Activity 2:

Target:
From/to.

Materials:
A clock with hands to manipulate; a sequence story of daily events.
Tell the story, using the clock to indicate the exact time:
'Peta got up at six o'clock. From six o'clock to seven o'clock she got dressed. From seven o'clock to half past seven she ate her breakfast...' Assist the child to repeat the story.
Other prepositions of time can be found in the chapter on Conjunctions and include: **when, while, till, until, since, before, after**. They may be used either in phrases:
Until morning, before breakfast;
or in clauses: When I come, while you wait, before breakfast.

Manner

With

Activity 1:

Target:
With.

Materials:
Model dolls or animals; some small items for the dolls to 'carry'.
Select two subjects. Activate them appropriately and model the target utterance:
Daddy is walking with Mommy.
The pig is walking with the cow.
Allow the child to manipulate the models and use the target utterance.

Variation:
Give the dolls objects to carry:
Mommy is walking with the bucket.
The boy is running with the ball.

Activity 2:

Target:
With.

Materials:
Pictures of a single subject with different attributes:
A boy with red pants
A boy with blue pants
A boy with dirty shoes
A boy with clean shoes
A monkey with a banana
A monkey with an orange
A monkey with a long tail
A monkey with a short tail
Turn the pictures face downwards and take turns identifying them one by one.
'(This is) the monkey with the banana' (see Post-modification, Book Two).

Activity 3:

Target:
With.

Materials:
A comb, a pen, a pair of scissors.
Ask:
'What do we do with a pair of scissors?'
The reply:
'Cut!'
You may insist on a full sentence in reply for the purpose of mastering the target, but remember it is not appropriate in a conversational context: 'I cut with a pair of scissors.'

For/from

Activity 4:

Target:
For/from.

Materials:
Tokens.
Take turns sharing out the tokens using the appropriate target utterance: 'This is for you/for me.'
'I take it from you' (see Activities to Teach Pronouns).

By

Activity 5:

Target:
By.

Materials:
Model vehicles; a map; model buildings or pictures of places such as: school, home, shops etc.
Instruct the child:
'Go to the shop.'
'Will you go by car, or by plane or by train?'
He will enjoy selecting a vehicle even if inappropriate, and must then reply using the target 'by plane'.

Deaf adolescents and learning-disabled children experience particular difficulty mastering a variety of prepositions. Quirk *et al.* (1972, pp.320-333) provide a comprehensive list of English prepositions, with detailed explanations of their meanings. They very aptly categorise these prepositions as detailed below. Here, selected from their list are those prepositions which we think might be useful for you to teach. We have not provided activities to teach these structures as there are excellent school grammars compiled for this purpose.

Additional prepositions

All over/throughout

The boy spilt milk all over the carpet.
He talked throughout (all through) the concert.

Metaphorical use of prepositions

Place

1) In/out of:
In/out of danger; in difficulties; to keep out of trouble; in books; in a group; in/out of the race.

2) Above/below/beneath:
To be above/below someone on a list; above/below one's income; such behaviour is beneath (not below) him; he's above such behaviour.

3) Under:
Under suspicion/orders; he has many people working under him.

4) Up/down:
Up/down the scale; up/down the social ladder.

5) Beyond/past/over:
Beyond/past endurance; beyond/past hope; beyond/past recovery; we're over the worst.

6) Between/amongst:
A fight/match between...; quarrel/agree among(st) ourselves; relationship/contrast between two things.

Duration

1) For:
We camped for the winter.
Idiomatic phrases include: for now, for ever, for good.

2) Over/through/throughout:
We camped there over the holidays.
We camped there through(out) the summer.

3) Between/by/up to from (preposition of time):
I'll phone you between one and four o'clock.
By the time you come; up to the end of term; I hadn't heard from him.

Cause

1) Prepositions used to denote cause, reason and motive:
Because of the examinations, I can't go out; for fear of being hurt; they were weak from lack of exercise; I do it out of pity; he ran the race for fun; I did it on account of my conscience.

2) Purpose, intended destination:
He'll do it for reward; they all ran for shelter; I'll give you lunch for school; he died for his country.

3) Recipient, goal, target:
He laid a trap for the rabbit.

Means

With/by/in:
He treated me with love and respect.
He shot the buck with a bow and arrow.
He managed to reach it with a long stick.
I go by bus.
He entered by the fanlight.
By steering the car carefully, he kept it from sliding on the ice.
The boy was knocked over by a bus.

Support or Opposition

For/with/against:
I'm with you in selecting that boy.
Go with the majority in making your decision.
Are you with/for/against the plan?

Post-modification of nouns

Of

Of phrases are the most commonly used in English:
A business of my father's; the cheek of the woman; the pride of the pack; the route of the explorers; the value of money; a herd of buffalo; a plate of soup; twelve of them; the people of Africa.

Having

Of, with, without:
A girl with a basket of apples (see 'with'– manner).
An employee without any faults.
A man of distinction.

Concession

In spite of, despite, for and all, with and all, notwithstanding:
I like that dog, in spite of its size.
Despite strong opposition, he will come.
With/for all his boasting, he can't do it.
John, notwithstanding his anger, has apologised.

Reference

With regard to, as for, as to:
With reference to your letter, I confirm our arrangement.
With regard to your holiday, the booking is confirmed.
As for Andrea, she's as busy as ever.
I value your comments as to what I should choose.

Exception

Except for, with the exception of:
We had a good holiday, except for the accommodation.
With the exception of Gary, they all came.
Everyone but me was tired.

Negative condition

But for:
But for Kenny, everyone was tired.

Subject matter

About, on:
He's speaking on the subject of History.
I'll find out about the party.

Ingredient, material

With, of, out of:
You make soup with carrots.
Lined with silk.
He made it out of wool.
The pig built a house of straw.
A heart of gold.

Respect, standard

At, for:
That dog is big for a poodle.
He's clever at building things.

Reaction

At, to:
I was surprised at her reply.
I laughed at her.
To my mind, she was rude.
It seemed to me she was angry.

Conclusion

What is it to engage in the task of teaching a child to communicate? Exhilarating, rewarding, challenging, satisfying, to the layman perhaps! But to the over-worked, anxious therapist and teacher, we could add the following description – frustrating, worrying, demanding and exhausting!

If you are conscientious about your work, it's a never-ending battle to keep abreast of current theoretical trends, while coping with heavy caseloads. Work-settings are often far from ideal. The 'ivory-tower' institution in which you trained seems to have been left far behind; the myriad of facts and theories you have been taught appear to have little relevance in the day-to-day interactions with your clients.

We are unable to offer you a panacea for your ills, and the writers acknowledge that they are but fellow-travellers on that rocky road to the attainment of excellence. We offer you what we hope are practical work books for the practising clinician. They are based on some current ideas about language development, and they incorporate models of syntactic development which are applicable to all children attempting to master the English language.

Normally-developing children are expected to master the grammatical forms we describe during their pre-school years. Delayed or deviant language learners may require this programme far beyond their early years, and with some consideration for chronological age and appropriate interests, all the activities described in the books are applicable to any age group.

This book has provided a basic description of English grammar, along with the systematic order in which to teach language forms. For the busy clinician and teacher, we hope that the inclusion of lists such as that of irregular past verbs, a comprehensive list of prepositions and a complete description of pronouns will be of real practical use.

Our intention, as already stated in the Introduction to the series, is to assist you in generating your own therapy. These are not 'recipe books'. If you practise the planning of lessons as we suggest in Book One, you will soon find yourself producing original and motivating language exercises. Remember – every target structure must be contextually relevant.

We have included the chapter on home visiting to remind you that children learn to communicate in a variety of contexts, but principally within the family setting.

No therapist can hope to be successful if her charges are not having fun. It is unnecessary to provide a wide variety of expensive toys, and we have suggested a limited number of materials to make or purchase, which should enable you to plan motivating therapy.

Some of our readers unfamiliar with language assessment may feel inadequate to plan and execute our programme. While, ideally, language specialists should always be involved in the teaching of language skills, the reality is that such specialists are very thin on the ground and their interests often exclude practical management. The demands of a large, culturally diverse clinical population require all of us to become involved, and to apply our skills to assist the communicatively-impaired child. Perhaps there is a language specialist in your district willing to assist you in assessing the children in your care. This will make programme planning easier and more relevant. Be encouraged by the fact that what you may lack in theoretical knowledge, you make up for in years of experience. However, this text will assist you to bring your work into line with current trends in language research. Try to organise seminars and workshops in your school or district. It is essential to role-play your therapy in advance and anticipate planning a contextually relevant exercise.

We have acknowledged that cultural differences must be considered in planning your programme. Materials must also be chosen in terms of cultural relevance and interest. It is hoped that our work will encourage others to provide relevant resource materials and activities for different cultural groups. The basic principles of language teaching remain the same. Similar texts to teach other language groups should also be developed. The programme or technique you adopt in order to attain your goal will always be refined and determined by your own unique presentation. This 'uniqueness' will be further refined by the needs and personalities of the children with whom you are working. You will change and adapt our programme, or some other one, in order to reach your goal. Your own work will be refined, defined and redefined as long as your struggle continues to impart that wondrous gift – human communication. We can but hope to have offered you yet another set of tools to increase your skills. An old Hindu proverb says : 'There is nothing noble in being superior to some other man. The true nobility is in being superior to your previous self.'

BIBLIOGRAPHY

ANDREWS, James R. and ANDREWS, Mary A. 1987. Remediation in the Family Context: Programmatic Models. New Orleans (Mini-seminar, American Speech-Language-Hearing Association Convention).

BANGS, Tina E. 1980. Instrumental Programming for Children with Language-Learning Disability. Detroit (Short Course, American-Speech- Language-Hearing Association Convention).

BATES, E. 1976. *Language in Context*. New York, Academic Press.

BLOCH, Donald A. 1974. An Introduction to Family Therapy. Johannesburg (Workshop under the auspices of Tara Hospital).

BLOOM, L.M. 1970. *Language Development: Form and Function in Emerging Grammars*. Cambridge, Mass., M.I.T. Press.

BOSCOLO, L. 1985. Family Therapy: The Milan Approach. Johannesburg, 3rd Biennial Conference, Marital and Family Therapy Association.

BUTLER, Katherine G. 1984. Language Processing: Halfway up the Down Staircase, in G. Wallach and K.G. Butler, *Language Learning Disabilities*. Baltimore, Williams and Wilkins.

─────── and SAWYER, Diane J. 1985. Language Links: At the Intersection of Spoken and Written Language. Washington (Short Course, American Speech-Language-Hearing Association Convention).

CONSTABLE, Catherine M. and VAN KLEECK, Anne 1985. From Social to Instructional Uses of Language: Bridging the Gap. Washington (Short Course, American Speech-Language-Hearing Association Convention).

COURTMAN-DAVIES, Mary 1979. *Your Deaf Child's Speech and Language*. London, The Bodley Head.

CRAWFORD, Louise 1979. Auditory Training: A Teacher's Approach, in Pat Vaughan (ed.), *Learning to Listen*. Ontario, Newspress.

CRYSTAL, David 1982. *Profiling Linguistic Ability*. London, Edward Arnold.

───────; FLETCHER, Paul and GARMAN, Michael 1976. *The Grammatical Analysis of Language Disability*. London, Edward Arnold.

DE MAIO, Louis J. 1983. A Communicatively Based Language Intervention Model for Young Children. Cincinatti (Short Course, American Speech-Language-Hearing Association Convention).

ECCARIUS, Melinda 1979. Cognitive Therapy. Unpublished Paper, Nebraska Boys Town Institute for Communication Disorders in Children.

EWALD, Carolyn 1985a. The Early Literacy Development of Young Deaf Children. Unpublished Paper, Gallaudet University for the Deaf, Washington D.C.

———— 1985b. The Language Approach to Facilitating Reading and Writing for Hearing-impaired Students. Unpublished Paper, Gallaudet University for the Deaf, Washington D.C.

FERGUSON, Charles A. 1977. Baby Talk as a Simplified Register, in Catherine Snow and Charles Ferguson (eds), Talking to Children. New York, Cambridge University Press.

GALLAGHER, Tanya M. 1983. Pre-Assessment: A Procedure for Accommodating Language Use Variability, in Tanya M. Gallagher and Carol A. Prutting (eds), Pragmatic Assessment and Intervention Issues in Language. San Diego, California College, Hill Press Inc.

GILLHAM, Bill 1979. The First Words Language Program. London, George Allen and Unwin; and Beaconsfield, Beaconsfield Publishers.

HALEY, J. 1973. Uncommon Therapy. New York, W. W. Norton.

HALLIDAY, M.A.K. 1973. Explorations in the Functions of Language. New York, Elsevier Holland Publishing Company.

HANNAH, Rosemarie P.; LIPPERT, Emily A. and HARRIS Ann B. 1982. Developmental Communication Curriculum. Columbus, Ohio, Charles E. Merril and A. Bell and Howell.

HUTTENLOCKER, Janellen 1971. Children's Language: Word-Phrase Relationship, in Aaron Bar-Adon and Werner F. Leopold (eds), Child Language: A Book of Readings. New Jersey, Prentice-Hall.

KRETSCHMER, Richard R. and KRETSCHMER, Laura W. 1978. Language Development and Intervention with the Hearing Impaired. Baltimore, University Park Press.

LAHEY, Margaret 1988. A Developmental Perspective for Assessing Children's Narratives (Short Course, American Speech-Language-Hearing Association Convention).

LASSMAN, Grace Harris 1950. Language for the Pre-School Deaf Child. New York, Grune and Stratton.

LEE, Laura L. 1974. Developmental Sentence Analysis. Evanston, Northwestern University Press.

LING, Daniel 1976. Speech and the Hearing Impaired Child: Theory and Practice. Washington D.C., The Alexander Graham Bell Association for the Deaf.

LUND, Nancy J. November 1987. Remediation in the Family Context: Programmatic Models. New Orleans (Mini-seminar, American Speech-Language-Hearing Association).

————and DUCHAN, Judith F. 1983. *Assessing Children's Language in Naturalistic Contexts*. New Jersey, Prentice-Hall.

LURIA, A.R. 1971. The Directive Function of Speech in Development and Dissolution, in A. Bar-Adon and W.F. Leopold (eds), *Child Language – A Book of Readings*. New Jersey, Prentice Hall.

LUTERMAN, David 1987. *Deafness in the Family*. New York, Little, Brown & Co.

MALLARD, A.R. 1987. The Use of Family Intervention in Stuttering: Therapy for Children. New Orleans (Mini-seminar, American Speech-Language-Hearing Association).

McCONKEY, Roy 1985. *Working with Parents – A Practical Guide for Teachers and Therapists*. London and Sydney, Croom Helm

MENYUK, Paula 1969. *Sentences Children Use*. Boston, M.I.T. Research Monograph No. 52.

————1971. *The Acquisition and the Development of Language*. New York, Prentice Hall.

————1972. *The Development of Speech*. New York, the Bobbs-Merril Company.

MILLER, J. 1981. *Assessing Language Production in Children: Experimental Procedures*. Baltimore, University Park Press.

MINUCHIN, S. 1974. *Families and Family Therapy*. Boston, Harvard University Press.

MINUCHIN, S. and FISHMAN, H.C. 1981. *Family Therapy Techniques*. New York, Harvard University Press.

MUMA, J. 1978. *Language Handbook: Concepts, Assessment and Intervention*. Englewood Cliffs, New Jersey, Prentice-Hall.

PHILLIPS, Juliet R. 1973. Syntax and Vocabulary of Mothers' Speech to Young Children: Age and Sex Comparisons. *Child Development* 44, pp.182-85.

PINK, M.A. and THOMAS, S.E. 1970. *English Grammar: Composition and Correspondence*. London, Cassell (12th edition).

PRUTTING, C.A. 1982. Pragmatics as social competence. *Journal of Speech and Hearing Disorders* 47, pp. 1, 23-134.

PRUTTING, Carol A. and KIRCHNER, Diane M. 1982. Applied Pragmatics, in T.M. Gallagher and C.A. Prutting (eds), *Pragmatic Assessment and Intervention Issues in Language*. San Diego, College Hill Press.

QUIRK, Randolph; GREENBAUM, Sidney; LEECH Geoffrey and SVARTVIK, Jan 1972. *A Grammar of Contemporary English*. Essex, Longman House.

ROMAINE, Suzanne 1984. *The Language of Children and Adolescents*. Oxford, Basil Blackwell.

RUDER, Kenneth F. and RICE, Mabel November 1978. Imitation, Comprehension and Production in Language Intervention. San Francisco (Short Course, American Speech-Hearing-Language Convention).

RUSTIN, Lena 1987. The Use of Family Intervention in Stuttering Therapy for Children. New Orleans (Mini-seminar, American Speech-Hearing-Language Convention).

SELIGMAN, Milton 1983. Siblings of Handicapped Persons, in Milton Seligman (ed.), *The Family with a Handicapped Child: Understanding and Treatment*. London, Grune and Stratton Ltd.

SIMMONS-MARTIN, Audrey 1976. A Demonstration of Home Approach with Hearing-Impaired Children, in Elizabeth Webster (ed.), *Professional Approaches with Parents of Handicapped Children*. Springfield, Charles C. Thomas.

SINOFF, A. 1985. Personal communication.

SLOBIN, D. 1975. On the Nature of Talking to Children, in Eric Lennenberg and Elizabeth H. Lennenberg (eds), *Foundations of Language Development: A Multidisciplinary Approach*, Vol. I. Paris, Academic Press and Unesco Press.

SNOW, Catherine E. 1977. Mother's Speech Research: From Input to Interaction, in Catherine E. Snow and Charles A. Ferguson, *Talking to Children*. Cambridge, Cambridge University Press.

TRANTHAM, C. and PETERSON, J. 1976. *Normal Language Development: The Key to Diagnosis and Therapy for Language Disordered Children*. Baltimore, Williams and Wilkins.

VORCE, Eleanor 1974. *Teaching Speech to Deaf Children*. Washington D.C., Alexander Graham Bell Association.

WEBSTER, Elizabeth J. 1977. *Counselling with Parents of Handicapped Children: Guidelines for Improving Communication*. New York, San Francisco and London, Grune and Stratton.

WILSON, Mary Sweig 1976. *The Wilson Expanded Syntax Program*. Cambridge, Mass., Educatores Publishing Service Inc.